D0482993

If you had nothing to overcome, you would soon
be overcome with complacency. Struggle keeps you
from apathy, which is a form of death, a way of
giving up on a situation or giving in to a problem.

Where There's A Wall There's A Way

DON H. POLSTON

LIVING BOOKS
Tyndale House Publishers, Inc.
Wheaton, Illinois

Scripture references are taken from *The Living Bible*,
unless otherwise noted.

First printing, Living Books edition, September 1985
Library of Congress Catalog Card Number 85-50951
ISBN 0-8423-8204-6

CONTENTS

ONE
Through Struggle and Stress 9
Conflicts Are to Be Conquered
Struggle Only Makes the Road Seem Long
Struggle Is the Secret for Survival
Take the Risk in Your Distress
When You Doubt, Develop
Faith Becomes Strong in the Storm

TWO
Life Bites and Blights, but Ignites 16
Life Bites
Difficulties Are Trampolines
Obstacles and Destinations
Possibilities in Hard Places
Problems Are Possibilities
What About Perennial Joy?
Adversity Is Part of Adventure

THREE
Problems Produce Progress 25
Grit = God + You
Life Is Rough
Jesus Was Tough
Convictions and Conflicts
Don't Commit These Days to the Devil
Life Is Not Easy
Courage Is Discovered in the Face of Despair
Death Is the Bottom Side of Life

FOUR

Anticipate Your Alterations 36

Amputated Dreams Hurt
Don't Hesitate to Make a Change When Necessary
Learning to Say Good-bye Is a Form of Amputation
Blend and Bend with Life to Avoid Being Broken
  by Life
What Do Mistakes Tell You?
Attitude Is Your Portfolio
Keep Adjusting the Dials

FIVE

Is There an Ouch in the House? 45

The Kid Most Like You
Kids Can Kill You
Call Your Kids
Divorce Is an Ouch!
Sex Is Sensational
The Woman Who Outruns Her Husband Runs Out
  of Husbands
Life Starts in Chaos

SIX

Create or Stagnate 53

Conformity Can Cripple You
Do You Really Need Their Approval?
Be True to You
When There Is None to Help—What Then?
The Dark Mind Defeats
Echoes Are Seldom Refreshing
Don't Depend Too Much on Others
Originals Are Usually Rejected—at First

SEVEN

When Things Don't Work Out—Work On   64

Is It Worth Your Effort?
What Will It Take to Send You Back?
The Waiting Room Is Hard
Solitude Is Sacred
The Secret of Performing
Work on Your Anxieties
Make Your Decisions Right Ones

EIGHT

Pessimism Pulverizes! 74

How to Make Yourself Miserable
How to Make Enemies
Getting Fat Takes Work
Negativism Gets What You Don't Want
How to Raise Criminals in the Home
How to Defeat Opportunity
Depression Deadens

NINE

What You See, Sees You 84

What You See, Sees You
Don't Worry About What You Missed
Develop Your Awareness
Build a New World
Let Nothing Stop You
What Will You Be Doing at Eighty-four?
Winter in the Soul
Problem-Spotting

TEN

Experiencing the Excitement of Failure .. 95

Everyone Needs to Experience Failure
Not All Failure Is Bad
Defeat Can Become a Way of Life
Success in Failure
Look for Your Fortunes in Your Misfortunes
Failing Courageously
Get Up Again
Start to Become

ELEVEN

The Tenderhearted and Tough-Minded   105

Tough but Tender
Don't Be Afraid of Them
Boost the Ego
The Good of Sorrow
Little People Need Big Things
Misplaced Because You're Misunderstood
Have You Been Misread?

TWELVE
Need Is Supply Knocking 114
The Key to the Supply Room
Give What You Need
Giving Is Receiving
Expectations Build Experiences
Everyone Needs Approval
Big Needs Demand Risk
Hoarding Leads to Poverty

THIRTEEN
Who's Who in the World of What's What   121
Who Are You?
Jesus Didn't Come to Prove a Point
Watch Out for Self-Rejection
How Jealousy Found Reality
The Disfigured Image
Deny Yourself
Free Spirit
How Do You See Yourself?

FOURTEEN
Hangovers Come from Hang-Ups 130
It All Seems So Unfair
Are You Up Against It?
No Problems, No Progress
How to Transform Your Troubles
Disadvantages Are Useful

ONE
Through Struggle and Stress

Life is not all struggle; nor is it always success. But life does bring conflicts and contests. Doubts batter you; battles bruise you. But in all of it, Christ offers you his own strength. You can succeed right where you are.

CONFLICTS ARE TO BE CONQUERED

You will read in books or hear in lectures, "Life can be free of conflict." But the Bible never says that. When Israel crossed the Jordan to enter the Promised Land, the conflicts became **greater.** It was a land of milk and honey, true. But it was also a land of battles and scars.

When Jesus said, "I am leaving you with a gift— peace of mind and heart!" (John 14:27), he was not promising there would be no more war. You need to learn how to win in war. Spotting land mines and recognizing the enemy are necessary skills for survival and happiness.

Each day, each moment, you may face a conflict to conquer. The conflicts may come from your first encounter of the day. The coffee is cold, the furnace is off, the car won't start, the garage door is stuck, or a dog scatters your garbage all over the street.

Deeper conflicts than these will come. Conflict with temptation, with people in general, or with your ineffective self will rise up and say, "I'm defeated."

Don't let conflicts cast you into a prison of despair. Once you believe the truth—that conflicts are a part of conquest—you will be on the winning side. Without conflicts, there is no crown. If there are no struggles, there are no successes. Ignore the problems and you will find no solutions. Only you can decide what kind of life you will live. Will you turn your conflicts into conquests, your chains into crowns? It's up to you!

STRUGGLE ONLY MAKES THE ROAD SEEM LONG

Are you tired of hoping? Does it appear your dreams will never come true? Are the answers long overdue? You can't hold out much longer, it seems. Welcome to life! God's "waiting rooms" are never easy.

God's prophets thought the day of prosperity would never come.

1. Noah thought it would never rain.
2. Moses thought he would never cross the Red Sea.
3. Abraham thought he would never see the child Isaac.
4. Hannah thought she would always be barren.

5. The disciples thought the third day would never come.
6. John the Baptist questioned Jesus: "Are you really the one we are waiting for, or shall we keep on looking?" (Matthew 11:3).

All through the ages, people like you and me have questioned, wondered, and walked in the darkness, hoping every minute the light would shine. While you are waiting for the light, keep your dreams alive. Make your plans—big plans! See the reality of the hope in your heart. And when you see it, seal it up.

Hold to your dreams until the dreams hold you. Get hold of some project that's big enough to keep your interest all your life. Get a grasp on something stronger than the fleeting ideas and projects that are here today and gone tomorrow. God loves to change our lives as we hold tight to great plans for his glory!

Invest your life in a project for God and others. Stay with it until it turns around to bless you too. Cast your bread upon the waters—it **will** return!

STRUGGLE IS THE SECRET FOR SURVIVAL

There is no end to conflicts in life. But stress is needed if you are to be kept from distress!

You may seek the perfect home, the perfect mate, the perfect job, the perfect church. But to your disillusionment, you find none. No matter where or with whom you live, there is conflict in your imperfect world. Like all of us, you become perplexed, provoked, and paralyzed.

11

This world is full of surprises, but they don't come in neat, little colored packages. They may arrive as tons of torment, or squeaky little voices, or a lighted fuse on a firecracker that could explode at any time.

You don't want to accept this, preferring to try to outrun the conflicts. But conflicts produce character; conflicts create convictions. Conflicts can build or destroy.

Songs are born in the sustained suffering of night. When the lights are off and darkness surrounds the soul, the little light within starts to shine. You cannot see such a light when the sun is at noonday; it must be dark for the light to shine.

If you had nothing to overcome, you would soon be overcome with complacency. Struggle keeps you from apathy, which is in fact a form of death, giving up on a situation or giving in to a problem.

Conflict is always superior to apathy. It at least lets you know you are still in contact with life. There is no guarantee in this world that you will ever be without conflict.

It is comforting to know that "there is someone in your hearts who is stronger than any evil teacher in this wicked world" (1 John 4:4). That's all you need to know as you face the continuing conflicts of life.

TAKE THE RISK IN YOUR DISTRESS

When there are no more risks, you are in danger of losing your greatest security: your need! Have you realized that your greatest asset is your liability?

I believe the Lord teaches faith to people who know their limitations. Faith toughens in emergencies. God does not get you out of all debt; he uses your debts to teach you faith.

The greater your desire and your dreams, the greater your need. I suppose the worst thing that could happen to you (in regard to your faith) is to have no reason to risk. Many people prefer security to the joy of risking.

But some people must have risk in their lives. You may be one of them. To find the unlimited, you will need the impossible. Make big plans. Little miracles follow little plans. Big hopes, big dreams, precede God's greatest gifts. No risk, no rescue.

Always remember, people who have a good story to tell are people who have lived through a difficult situation. Start something for God that involves a risk, and he will rescue you every time. But his rescue comes through pressure, problems, and prayer.

WHEN YOU DOUBT, DEVELOP

Doubts are not in themselves wrong if you keep moving ahead. Some use the simple cliche, "If you doubt, don't." But let me give you a better one: "When you doubt, develop."

The only disciple who walked on the water with Jesus had definite doubts, but he moved over the side of the boat anyway and became known as a bold apostle of Christ. I'm not as ashamed of Peter, who nearly drowned when he saw the waves, as I am of the rest who never walked on the water or even made the attempt.

Peter had his doubts, but he stepped over the side of the boat into a treacherous sea. He at least made the attempt. None of the others in the boat could say they were rescued by the Savior from the stormy waters as Peter was.

The winning person is the one who keeps going over the side of the boat in the face of his doubts. I think if Peter had been given another opportunity, he would have walked on the water again. I think he would have said, "I doubted before, but let's try once more."

The very fact that I am well in body is evidence I have overcome disease and germs. My faith is proof I have at this time overcome the disease of doubt.

Each day I must conquer germs of doubt. They come at me each day, but my living cells must be stronger than the diseased cells if I am to stay healthy.

You must develop the power to move ahead, to keep going. Perseverance kills the germ of doubt.

Doubt your doubts, and have faith in your faith.

Your life is at its best when it is fully committed to a project, an idea, or a concept in spite of the doubts. Move ahead in the face of doubt. This is the way faith is fashioned and becomes fully grown.

Stress gives birth to success in the face of doubts if you keep moving ahead with Christ.

FAITH BECOMES STRONG IN THE STORM

There will always be storms ahead of you in this life. No matter what size storm you face, use your faith. No matter how small your faith is, put it to work.

Little faith becomes great faith as you use it in

the storms of life. What you don't use, you lose. Don't condemn yourself for the size of your faith. You simply have not risked enough to make the faith you already have grow stronger.

Take the faith you now possess and use it by affirming what the Bible says about you and your situation. If you lack, say, "[God] . . . will supply all [my] needs" (Philippians 4:19). If you are hurting, say, "The Lord comforted me so I can comfort someone else" (see 2 Corinthians 1:4). Share with others what God's revelation has shown you.

Faith is tough; it is not weak. It can endure. It can hang on long after reason has deserted it.

Your faith may be small, but it's tough. Doubts can't kill it; man can't take it away from you; sickness cannot hold it back. Sorrow and poverty can actually cause it to grow. God is at work in you!

What can kill God? Nothing! Who can defeat the Lord? No one! All faith is from God. If you misuse it, you will suffer the consequences of unbelief. If you work with it, you will reap a glorious harvest of spiritual fruit.

Faith is made strong only in storms. Strength comes out of struggle. Faith bears fruit in the close encounters of battle.

Through struggle and stress—perhaps because of them—you will succeed.

T W O

Life Bites and Blights, but Ignites

Jesus never promised an easy road as you work and walk with him. Life hurts, harms, and hinders. Only the few who understand and accept this struggle on to success. There is rest in the presence of restlessness and contentment in the midst of conflicts. Learn this and you will be ready for true success.

LIFE BITES

Joyce Landorf, speaking at our annual Winning Woman's Retreat, said explosively, "Life bites." And she is right! There are times when the teeth of reality take a painful hunk out of your emotions or imagination. You are left stunned and shocked from the unexpected bite.

We live in a world of blows and billows as well as blessings, and all come when you don't seem to expect them. You, like all of us, may cry, "Why me? What have I done? I don't deserve this!" And probably you didn't, but it came anyway. I don't know that it came to improve you as much as to prove you.

Proving is always harder on us than improving! It's nice to think you are improving (though it's always so slow). But it's tough to know you are being proven, which of necessity includes being tested. Trials prove your faith; they test its fiber.

When life bites, it seems unfair. Jesus honestly heralded this unwanted truth in the words, "Here on earth you will have many trials and sorrows" (John 16:33). Who wants to hear that? Let's talk about trophies and triumphs. But the trophies and the triumphs are the result, not the cause, of tribulations. The rewards come after the race—so keep running!

The only consolation you have when life bites is the words of Christ: "I have overcome the world" (John 16:33). You can overcome too, if you refuse to be overcome, but instead persevere in Christ.

Life bites, true. But don't be surprised—be strong.

DIFFICULTIES ARE TRAMPOLINES

Disappointments can be trampolines from which you bounce back to life and strength. The Bible says, "Those who sow tears shall reap joy" (Psalm 126:5). It also tells us, "[God] placed springs in the valleys" (Psalm 104:10).

Water in the valley
light in the darkness
hope in despair
deliverance in defeat—this is the secret.

Faith looks at the usual in an unusual way. It takes the ordinary and discovers its true meaning. How you see a thing determines what you do with it, as well as what it does to you.

Tears are an unavoidable part of life. The tears of trouble fill your cup. But the tears you sow are preparing you for a harvest of joy. Out of your problems will rise power, if you allow it to be so. Look at your problem with an eye of faith. See it from many sides. See if there is another way to use it. The greatest test could become your greatest triumph.

Go back to the beginning. Reexamine the situation. See where it all started, and then you can correct it. Every corrected problem is another stone in the foundation of your life and growth.

Whatever you do, don't lose faith in yourself or in your God. God can do nothing more for you if you lose faith in his ability and availability. The next time trouble hits, make it a trampoline to bounce you to higher levels of life.

OBSTACLES AND DESTINATIONS

Obstacles must be overcome if they stand between you and your destination. Where are you going? What must you overcome to get there? Are you willing to pay the price? If obstacles are not removed, you will not grow or succeed.

Continually trying to go around your obstacles will wear your hopes out. You must find a way to remove or surmount whatever barrier you face. The difference between reaching goals and not reaching them is your ability to meet and master the situation.

The Jordan River lay between the misery of the wilderness and the joy of the Promised Land for Joshua and the people of God. There was no alternative but to cross it. They stepped into the water and went over their obstacle onto dry land.

When I was writing this chapter, I had been going through some difficulties. I was deeply depressed and seemingly faced an insurmountable problem. Then this encouraging word came to me from an eighty-four-year-old German man whom I'd never met: "Accept the things you cannot change and just keep going on. Remember, the woods are full of people who would try to hinder you. Don't be discouraged."

This did it, and I did it. My new friend's words helped me climb my mountains.

The next time you are facing the bites and blights of life, look for an encouraging word. It may come from a book or perhaps from an old, insignificant-looking person who is God's messenger to you.

Whatever you do, don't wear your hopes out going around and around your obstacles. Go over them with God's help.

POSSIBILITIES IN HARD PLACES

The most difficult circumstances contain possibilities for progress and growth.

My television and radio director brings problems to me almost weekly. But he recognizes that all these problems have answers. "I don't discuss these problems with you, Pastor, as if there is no solution to them. I only talk about them because I know there's a way through," he says with a gleam of hope in his eye.

The problems will always be there. When you solve one, you create another. But remember this: you can learn to see through your problems to the answers; you can always find a way.

Jesus asked his disciples, "Where can we buy bread to feed all these people?" (He already knew what he would do. The question was for the disciples' benefit.) Then Andrew's answer came: "There's a youngster here with five barley loaves and a couple of fish! But what good is that with all this mob?" (see John 6:5-9). Jesus saw a way through. He saw past the empty purse and the skimpy groceries. He saw the possibility in a hard place. Consequently, he was able to feed the people.

All through the Bible you can find people who saw possibilities while others only saw perplexing situations. Wondrous miracles always follow the steps of a person who refuses to be trapped by hard circumstances. He uses hard stones to build bridges over troubled waters.

Winners and overcomers persevere in the face of difficult circumstances. They find a way. They use a problem as a stepping-stone to a new level of life.

PROBLEMS ARE POSSIBILITIES

You will always face some kind of problem needing to be solved. And that's good, because problems indicate needs. When you have a problem, you have a need; and when you have a need, you have a problem.

Problems are also possibilities in waiting. What

you do with them could determine your future.

Your family may have a need, or maybe it's your home or business. Who can meet that need? Solving a problem becomes the source of meeting the need. What you solve becomes your servant.

Usually your need will be met by a united effort as you work in cooperation with others. The Bible clearly states, "My God shall supply all your need" (Philippians 4:19, KJV). This is true. But God does this in many ways and through many channels. He brings people, ideas, and pressures into your world, hoping you will see them as means through which your needs are being met.

Some means God uses may not be very enjoyable to you, but he knows what he is doing. He sends this book, that new friend, or that financial situation into your life to meet your needs by providing ideas or inspiration. He works his miracles through people and circumstances. Hopes, problems, and even crises give God the chance to prove himself to you.

God can only reconfirm his good intentions for you if you have a pressing need. Delight in your need; thank God for it. "Dear brothers, is your life full of difficulties and temptations? Then be happy, for when the way is rough, your patience has a chance to grow" (James 1:2, 3).

Whatever you are not able to bear, God will take upon himself. If your problem becomes too great, cast it on Jesus. No matter what you face, you can cope with it in his power, peace, and assurance. God is always with those who have received his Son as Savior.

Problems come, but God is there. He stands with you in your hurts. The problems of life give the opportunity to work with God in solving the difficulties and so find an unlimited source of strength and wisdom.

To many, problems necessarily mean a lack of joy. People panic under pressure. But each time you panic, you lose. Once you understand, at least a little, God's purpose for allowing the problem or trial, you will be able to handle it.

WHAT ABOUT PERENNIAL JOY?

But let's be realistic: maintaining constant joy or peace of mind is almost impossible as you seek to develop the ability to work through your problems. There will be a thousand undermining attacks, sometimes gradual and sometimes instantaneous, which destroy your present peace of mind.

Whenever a heaviness settles on you, there will be a temporary loss of joy and sense of well-being. This heaviness can do two things for you:

1. It can drive you into yourself and away from people.
2. Or it can sharpen your insights to life and godliness.

The bites and blows of life can turn you on to new thoughts or can turn you aside from pursuing your goals. If you expect to win in this world, you must learn to experience and control these deadening and numbing feelings.

Some losses are really gains, and some gains are actually losses.

At a moment of loss, it may look as if all things are gone—all your joy, hope, creativity. But the steady soul rebounds from seeming defeat and accepts resurrection to new insights and commitments gained through the loss. No one can appreciate success unless they have experienced defeat.

Don't hang your hat on a rack of perennial joy. It can change in a moment. Instead, rely on the presence of God. If joy is clouded by sorrow and misunderstanding, remember that it will return. The sun may set, but it will come up again. There is no darkness that the light cannot penetrate.

The waves rise and fall but the ocean remains. The darkness comes and goes, but the light never goes out, because you cannot be separated from God's love.

ADVERSITY IS PART OF ADVENTURE

No adversity—no adventure. Whatever you are up against could indicate that you are near a turningpoint in your adversity.

Opposition could mean you are on the right road. Yet, we often look for an easy path as we journey down the road of life. We seek the key that easily unlocks the door to success. We naturally, but incorrectly, think that the hard way is the wrong way.

The universe is built on opposites, and this is the reason for opposition in life. Someone has said, "I judge the worth of what I'm doing by the opposition it encounters."

Adversity is part of adventure; criticism is par for the course. Learn to live with it.

The weak fall back when opposition of one kind

23

or another comes against them. If you want to progress, you will have to do so under the fire of opposition. There will never be a time when all things will be just right for you to do your best. You must learn to do your best when life is at its worst. This is the difference between a winner and a loser.

Opposition strengthens your talents, builds your faith, develops your courage, and causes you to trust in God. Peter said, "Don't be bewildered or surprised when you go through the fiery trials ahead" (1 Peter 4:12).

The next time you feel life has taken a bite or left a blight, just remember that life can be ignited too. Turn up the dial. Set the spark. Tell God you are willing to see possibilities in the hard places. Start today to uncover the possibilities in your problems.

Be strong in the Lord!

THREE
Problems Produce Progress

It's not always easy to become the person you want to be or to achieve the things you desire in life. There are people who hinder, problems to untangle, fears to overcome. In this chapter you will discover that problems produce either progress or defeat. **The courage to be you** is tough to build, but courage is the cornerstone of character.

GRIT = GOD + YOU

Grit is the courage to go on in the face of difficulties and obstacles, and very few people have it. Very few go on when the odds are against them. The world is full of people who have parked on the shoulder of life's roadway and will attack anyone who seeks to show them the way through their situation. They can give dozens of reasons why they have stopped building their world. They have let their problems paralyze them. Lacking grit, they quit.

Charles Jones lists these reasons for quitting:

1. I want to talk it over with my wife.
2. It isn't worth it.
3. I need to get away from it all.
4. No one understands me.
5. I don't have any title.
6. I don't have the personality.
7. I'm a self-made man.
8. I'm trying to find what I would like to do.

Grit is God plus you. Grit is the result of meeting God, learning what he wants you to do, and then doing it. Grit is not natural; it must be developed. It is the result of rejection, rebuffs, and rewards.

Once you understand rejection, you can conquer it. This is somewhat like a mouse seeking his way through a maze. Each electrical "reject" hurts, but the shock tells him he has to find another way. If one way or a thousand ways don't work, he still knows there's a way somewhere. With that assurance, he keeps trying until he finds the way through.

Grit is God plus you. So stand up, speak up, and stretch for success. Learn to cope with your hope!

LIFE IS ROUGH

Accept the fact that life is rough at times! If you realize this, you will seldom fall into a trap of self-pity. In your lifetime hostility, rejection, and deceit will be cast in your direction. Life on this earth will never be easy.

I remember a time when our church had been going through some very deep waters for over three years. It seemed we had fightings without and fears within. Each problem seemed to grow to monstrous proportions. People left. My ministerial leadership was questioned. I didn't know if I could stand much more. My wife turned to me one Sunday afternoon and said wistfully, "Will these struggles and problems ever cease? Can't we be fully accepted and loved for what we are and what we are doing?"

I hated to tell her the truth, but I had to. I reminded her that Paul was considered a castaway, and that Jesus was crucified. "If they hated Paul and Jesus, they will hate you," I said. I wanted Ruth Ann to see and face the reality of this problem-packed world. Jesus said, "Here on earth you will have many trials and sorrows" (John 16:33).

We cannot escape people's criticism, questioning, and rejection, but we can learn how to take it and go on.

Face all of life with courage and faith in God. You will stumble and make mistakes, and your enemies will take pleasure in your losses. But never retaliate. Be glad for the good, wherever you find it; and be helpful to the unworthy, wherever you find them.

Hate no one, not even the members of your family. (At times it is easier to love a stranger than the members of your own home.) **Love all.**

Love is not synonymous with approval. Love is a willingness to help.

The worst that could happen will happen to you at times. No one else will think it's the worst, because it has not happened to them or it's not their problem. Conversely, you may think everybody else's problems look easier than yours, just as to them your problems look easier than theirs. Sure, life is rough at times, filled with hostility and rejection; but remember that life is filled with adventure for the adventurous.

Life is only dull to the dull.

Life is only interesting to the interested.

Life is rough, but it's also rewarding to God's finders.

JESUS WAS TOUGH

Learn to speak up to your world. When the Pharisees said to Jesus, "You have a devil," he answered them boldly. He went so far as to say, "You are of your father the devil" (see John 7:20; 8:44, KJV).

Jesus felt rejection, revenge, and reproach. He knew about living like a lamb among wolves. But he seldom let others push him around without an answer; he knew how to stand up to his enemies. He accepted the cross when **he** was ready.

The Christian image today is often one of weakness, not meekness. Meekness has might. It has strength. It is not afraid to be itself.

Speak up to your world. Stand up to your problems. This does not mean you need to bully your way through. It simply means you must fully believe in who you are in Christ and what you **can** do.

Bowing to the world to get its applause could mean failure. Stand tall in your heart. Compromise only turns people against you.

A subtle but safe rule is, don't overdo anything. The person who finds the balanced life finds great success.

The next time you are tempted to crawl, remember who you are—a child of God. Remain faithful to him.

Don't apologize for being on this planet. God planted you here for a purpose. If you don't take your place in this world, somebody else less capable will.

CONVICTIONS AND CONFLICTS

There will never be a time in your life when all you do or attempt to do will feel absolutely correct. Wait to be absolutely correct before you move and you will do or accomplish nothing.

One man said, "I **do** have faith; oh, help me to have **more!**" (Mark 9:24). He said it just right.

Even Jesus, when praying in the Garden of Gethsemane, cried out, "Father, if you are willing, please take away this cup of horror from me. But I want your will, not mine" (Luke 22:42).

Conviction and conflict both build character. Conviction says, "I will do it; I must do it." Contradiction or conflict says, "But what if I fail—what if I'm wrong? What if it doesn't work out?"

There has never been, nor will there ever be a person who has struck a new note, published a new book, or conceived a new child that hasn't at some time been bothered with doubts.

It is neither unnatural nor wrong to have conflict along with conviction. You can be committed and at the same time recognize the possibility that you may be wrong concerning something you presume to be good. This is the chance you must take.

There is no guarantee that what you are attempting will happen. But it is guaranteed that if you don't attempt it, you'll never do it. It is better to be sorry you failed in your effort than to find out the idea succeeded through another's efforts while you stood back and did nothing.

People with trophies say, "I'm not sure, but I'm moving ahead anyway. My convictions are not without conflicts, but I'll keep believing. My faith is beset by doubts, but I will still trust God."

Risk-takers are rewarded sooner or later.

DON'T COMMIT THESE DAYS TO THE DEVIL

The greatest days of your life are just ahead of you. Don't commit them to the devil.

It's a cop-out to accept these crisis days because of the coming Great Tribulation. The Tribulation may be near, but your transformation may be nearer.

What if you were standing on the stage of the greatest show on earth? How much more interest would you show if you thought you were in the play? Well, you are!

This generation has gone through troubles, testing, sins, and sorrows. We have been plagued with:

    power status
    popular songs
    preaching shows
    prosperity signs
    perverted saints
    perplexed sex
    political stress
    population statistics.

The curtain is already up!
The harvest is at hand.

Don't wait for the Great Tribulation; get into God's act today.

God's power can come to you only through a channel which you have opened. Enlarge your channel! Make it big at the inlet, and the outlet will be even greater.

This could be your greatest day.

LIFE IS NOT EASY

Life cannot be easy. If it is, you are not doing anything meaningful or going anywhere significant.

You are a builder, and building is tough work. Life outside God's care is not only difficult, but meaningless as well.

Why the struggle? Why the effort? There is no valid answer to these questions apart from the purposes of Christ being fulfilled in you.

God has given you many aids to help you handle difficulties in life: faith, prayer, endurance, grace, grit. You have intelligence—thank God for that. All the power of the universe will back you if you are true to yourself, your dreams, and your God. The good you seek will come to you in time.

On one occasion the disciples were in a storm on the Sea of Galilee and finally "arrived at the other side of the lake" (Mark 5:1). It seemed to them they would never make it, but with Christ in the boat they reached their goal. You, too, will arrive at your destination, even though you are going through a raging storm.

Life is sometimes tumultuous, but somehow, sometime you arrive. You reach the other side of your troubles. And when you arrive, you know it!

31

But arrival assumes a departure. Each valley has a mountain, and each mountain a valley. Your road will make one turn after another before it gets through the mountains.

When I was traveling in Switzerland, I thought the bus would never stop making sharp turns, going around tedious curves, and running through long, dark tunnels before we reached the top of the pass. We finally arrived, only to start the process again on the other side of the pass. The route was beautiful beyond description, but it was difficult too. As we came into Lucerne, a city on a lake, I was exhausted, excited, and now an experienced tour guide.

There was no way to make that trip any less difficult. But I am glad I didn't miss the experience under the excuse that it might be exhausting. Exhausting it was, but enduring it will remain.

That's the way life is.

COURAGE IS DISCOVERED IN THE FACE OF DESPAIR

If there is nothing to fear, courage collapses. Courage comes to life only in the presence of fear.

You must develop courage in order to create. How often have you wanted to write a book, cook a new dish, build a home, or travel to a foreign country, but allowed fear to overcome your good intentions? Fear made you fail to carry out these creations.

Perhaps you allowed despair, defeat, or general conditions of lack to hold you back from creativity. You may have looked over the past and concluded your family never reached certain goals—why should you?

The fact is, you don't know what your true potential is until you try. Courage is developed in the face of despair and need.

You would not need courage if there was nothing to fear. Courage is not the absence of fear or the absence of need; but in overcoming both, courage is born. Whoever restrains courage within himself, refusing to face new battles and blessings, experiences a type of death. Reasons for fear are calls for faith. Having nothing to overcome—this produces underachievers! Courage means moving ahead in the face of all opposition and difficulties.

Listen to your heart the next time you are afraid to express your ideas or concepts. It will tell you to try. The best friend you have is within you. "Christ in your hearts is your only hope of glory" (Colossians 1:27). He always pushes you forward; he encourages you to believe in who you are and what you must do.

Your best friend is you as you trust in Christ while facing conflict and building courage.

DEATH IS THE BOTTOM SIDE OF LIFE

Some have found that the older they grow, the less they fear death, because they have lived long enough to know there are some things in life worse than death. Also, they have learned that people, problems, and pressures can't kill you if you decide they won't. For the true Christian, death will be a welcome relief from the petty problems of this life. Gazing across the river to a land free from the struggles on Planet Earth brings joyful anticipation.

You **will** die. Death is the unavoidable termination

of life on this planet. As flowers and fruit die each autumn, you too ripen for death. You are being prepared for another life.

Is death to be feared, or should death be looked upon with joy? Paul asked: "O death, where then your victory? Where then your sting?" (1 Corinthians 15:55). Death once held a sting for us, but in Christ the sting is gone. Jesus took it out through his own death. He left us only the resurrection.

Is there life after death? Are there other people somewhere in the uncounted galaxies of the universe? Do they die too? Is death the only method for people to leave this planet and enter another? We don't know. But we do know this: death is a part of life for us.

God wants to bring us into a greater life through the door, Christ. Jesus said, "I am the door" (John 10:9, KJV).

We fear death because we are uncertain of the road beyond. We have not yet traveled that road. Yet, we **are** on that road, because the road of death is the road of life and the road of life is the road of death. They are the same. One is the beginning, the other the end.

You do not know when the end of your road will be. But Jesus has gone ahead, and that is enough. How many angels will be at your side when you die? I don't know. But I know this—Christ will be there, and that's sufficient.

Death will come when he sends it, and we'll be ready because he will make us ready.

Death will end my life here, but will begin my life in some better place, with God.

While he is preparing,
   I am growing
Through the problems.

He is the living Presence
   While I'm dying
Only to find **life.**

He is coming soon;
   I am going
Later to join them all.

While I am gone,
   You keep growing
Through your problems.

We shall meet
   again somewhere—
But complete!

FOUR

Anticipate Your Alterations

There are many amputations in life. Before you reach your goals, you will "lose" many people, places, and problems. Each amputation hurts, as your ambitions are cut off and your dreams are detoured. But great power will be yours if you keep the right attitude. And you can do this only if you bank on God's love, if you remember he is **for** you.

AMPUTATED DREAMS HURT

At times your greatest ambitions will be ruined by the attitudes and actions of unthoughtful people. What can you do when everything goes wrong?

Some days all your plans go astray. But is that so terrible? Isn't a greater mind, the mind of a loving God, at work in your plans even when they go sour? Can't your trials be used by God for your good?

The happy person is able to find good in the bad times. That's a good habit to develop, because oftentimes the good appears to have been overcome by the bad.

When things go wrong, **do not panic**. There is a tendency to run, give up, or fight when your plans fall apart. What do you do when people you trust walk out on you or seem to work against your life's plans? Have you ever realized this could be a blessing? As you grow toward being the man or woman God meant you to be, there will be times when people, places, and things are no longer good for **you**, and the only way for you to go on and grow on is for them to go away. Amputation always hurts, but many times it's really for the best.

Trust the God who lives in you. Be bold enough to believe he is leading you. If some things fall out of your life, recognize that it may be for the best. Let nothing but God be truly important to you. There is only one indispensable relationship—you and God.

Hold firmly to this, and all the rest will fall perfectly into place in your world. Anticipate amputation, and the alterations won't take you by surprise. Detours are part of the landscape; changes must come. When you learn to live with change, you will have a better chance to reach your potential.

DON'T HESITATE TO MAKE A CHANGE WHEN NECESSARY

A switch might do you good. If you are to become who you are really meant to be, you must let the unlimited desires boiling within your heart come out. To know the depths, you must go where it's deep.

How much are you worth? How much is your dream worth? How much are your prayers worth? What price tag would you put on yourself? Do you really know what you like to do? What can you do that is good for you and others?

Whatever you like to do, and can do honestly, that's what you should concentrate on and begin doing today. You don't need money. All you need is desire, a plan, and the courage to put it into action. Begin now—today!

"Like-to" is a divine indicator. That's why you have "like-to" in you. You don't need to want to do what others are doing in order to be "dedicated." Seek God's will, and do what you like to do. That's God's method in your life.

Nobody can do all the jobs on the earth. This is why we have pastors, doctors, teachers, workmen, wives, and mothers. Everybody has something he or she likes to do. Find out where you fit, and don't be afraid of change.

There will be plenty of times in your development when the amputations of life will not be made by appointment, but through disappointment. Realistically, you might not make the change necessary for your greatest good except through failures and trials. In his own wisdom, God uses disappointments to make room for his greater appointments.

LEARNING TO SAY GOOD-BYE IS A FORM OF AMPUTATION

You probably say good-bye to something or someone each day of your life. You're always arriving and departing. There are no permanent places or positions in this world.

Abraham spoke of his days on earth as a pilgrimage. He saw his life as a sojourn, for he had no permanent dwelling place. He left all to find all.

Learning how to say good-bye is important. The baby says good-bye to the womb at birth. The child says good-bye to the classroom when he graduates. Youth say good-bye to parents on their wedding day. And death calls us all to say good-bye to each other.

Jesus said good-bye to the disciples at his ascension. Paul said good-bye to the elders from the church at Ephesus. Whether we like it or not, learning to say good-bye becomes a way of life for all of us.

Life is pushing us forward every moment. It will not allow us to hold time or experience in a box for future pleasure or pursuits. We must deal with each moment of life.

Life is not stationary. The sun moves; the earth rotates; the next generation comes to take our place. We all say good-bye so very soon.

At some point in time, you will say good-bye to delights and joys, disappointments and defeats. Most of us have hidden away some certificates of disappointment. They have no real value to us—except that they teach us what **not** to do. We keep them around to remind us not to forget the lessons we've learned. Today put all of your life's hurts and disappointments together and say good-bye to them.

Learn to say good-bye, and so discover how to say hello to your coming world.

BLEND AND BEND WITH LIFE TO AVOID BEING BROKEN BY LIFE

Don't expect life to be the same each day. It won't be. Life is a blend, a mixture of good and bad, a combination of sweet and sour, joy and sorrow. There are days when the sun refuses to shine on your little world, and the darkness seems to refuse to go away. The sun goes down over your backyard, seemingly never to rise again.

There are other days though when the sun is brighter than ever, and you have the mistaken notion the shadows will never touch your life again. All pains are gone. The world is a picnic. Romance and adventure kiss each other. At last you think you have found paradise on this planet. I wish this were true, but it most certainly is not.

Life consists of bending and blending. It is a combination of tears, trophies, and tragedies, of losses and gains. The person who understands this has taken a giant step toward successful living. He has learned to use life as it is. When bruises come, he does not panic; when blessings arrive, he does not parade. He knows it can all change in a moment.

Sameness of life is a myth. God's Word causes both light and darkness to stand out! "The more we see our sinfulness, the more we see God's abounding grace forgiving us" (Romans 5:20). It takes the one to magnify the other.

Pain makes pleasure more enjoyable. Darkness

40

enhances light. Success is sweet when it is won in the face of loss.

What you have to overcome in order to gain makes the gain even more precious. Overcoming battles makes the victories even sweeter.

Thank God life is not the same each day. The blending of life makes life beautiful, and bending with life makes us stronger.

Let wind come—I'll use it to fill my sails. Let mistakes come—I'll use them to make me wise. Let disappointments come—I'll make them my appointments with God. Let death come—it is the gate to eternal life with God.

I don't want my days to all be the same. Let them change like the colors of fall and spring, for out of this change comes beauty in the soul.

WHAT DO MISTAKES TELL YOU?

A mistake tells you to try again. It indicates a need for improvement. It is not a getting-off place in the battle for survival, but a starting place for new growth. Start again whenever you fail.

Mistakes can teach you or terrorize you. They have the power to propel or paralyze you. They can finish you if you let them. The ditches on life's road are filled with the wreckage of people's ideas and dreams—because they allowed a mistake to take their eyes off their goal.

When you err, examine your mistake and see where you can change. Most likely the needed change will involve the mind before it involves the method. A method of living, coping, or whatever can be only as good as the mind that thought of it. A knowledge of one's mistakes is beneficial to the mind that is willing to try again.

Never give up because of your mistakes. Always keep in mind that if there is a wrong way to do something, there is also a right way. And you can find the right by learning from the wrong. In learning how not to live, you discover how to live.

Cut off your mistakes like you would an incurably diseased finger. Bury your mistakes; forget them and move on.

Experience is a tough teacher, but learning by hard knocks brings unforgettable knowledge.

ATTITUDE IS YOUR PORTFOLIO

Your attitude is more important than your attainments.

Actually, attainments are a reflection of attitude. All your attainments could become worthless in a day; but if your attitude is sound, it is only a matter of time until the same attainments are arrived at again.

Attitude is your checkbook, your portfolio, vitamins in your blood. Amputate your bad attitudes; let Christ replace them with better ones, ones more like his.

The single greatest weapon you have is your attitude. It affects how you pray. It governs what you do. Attitude can lift you off the ground like a jet engine or slam you into the ground like a falling spaceship.

Your attitude is the direct result of the daily pressures you face. Whatever things push against you will strengthen and establish your attitude. Your attitude is established by pressure—and by praise. The next time you feel a rotten attitude coming on, open your mouth wide and praise God for the situation. Praising him will send demons of defeat out of your life.

Attitude—the way you think, imagine, and reason —is sound when you center it on the Bible. Believe what the Bible says, and repeat it no matter what you see or how you feel. Repetition of God's promises establishes a good attitude. The Bible says, "Think on these things" (Philippians 4:8, KJV).

Attitude is everything. It's a shield in the battles of life, medication for wounds received from others. It's protection from the pitfalls of pressures. "We have the mind of Christ" (1 Corinthians 2:16, KJV). Let his attitude become yours.

KEEP ADJUSTING THE DIALS

You can never be wrong and still enjoy the right. If you are serious about being all you can be, you must give up dishonesty, all wrong, all selfishness.

Wrong goes against the grain, and the longer we hold to the wrong ways, the more difficult life becomes.

As you seek to excel, you must keep short accounts with God and so remain free from the burden of guilt. The power of guilt is beyond description. The free heart is the creating heart.

You will need to frequently adjust the dials of your heart and mind in order to stay in tune with God and life. He is the focal point. Only through his Spirit can you stay in tune with reality.

The success of your life depends upon these things: (1) knowing God; (2) keeping in touch with God; (3) giving yourself to others; (4) valid expectations.

Many times you will not know what is right unless you understand what is wrong. But if you do not want to know the right way to accomplish a thing, you will miss the mark. Being wrong, if you see that you are wrong, can help you see the right. The crucial question is, are you willing to change?

The Bible says, "Where sin abounded, grace did much more abound" (Romans 5:20, KJV). Darkness calls for light; cold calls for heat; sin calls for a Savior.

You will find the right when you admit you are wrong.

FIVE

Is There an Ouch in the House?

Many homes have experienced an "ouch" in the house.

The kid you rejected turned out to be most like you.

Divorce hit when you didn't suspect it.

The joys of sex turned sour.

The liberated wife was no longer needed by her husband.

The chaos of your house can be turned into a cosmos of order and beauty by the power of Christ. But building (or rebuilding) always starts at the bottom.

THE KID MOST LIKE YOU

Here's a basic truth: the more your kids have your characteristics, the more you will reject them. The things you don't like about yourself are what you don't like about your kids.

Books, lectures, seminars, sermons, films, re-
treats, small groups, large groups, and all kinds and
sizes of specialists tell you "how to have a happy
home." Most of these people share secrets learned
through their own failures. Some experts have in
fact "dropped out" when life with their kids was a
struggle.

If you are going to learn how to live life, you are
going to learn it in your own backyard. This does
not mean others cannot help you. They can. But
no one can fill your shoes. When the celebrity speakers are through, you are left right where you
started—on your own. If you mess up, it will be
your failure, not theirs. If you put it together and
make it work, it will be because of your willingness
and ability to make the effort.

No two homes are alike; don't copy someone
else. No two people are created the same. You are
unique. Don't panic if you're not like someone else.

Your home reflects you. What you are—that is
where you must begin.

Build your base of life on honesty, truth, love,
and the Word of God. Face needed alterations with
courage and hope. Allow time for the good to grow.
Plant seeds of understanding and reap their rewards, which will be more understanding. What you
plant, you will harvest. Keep at it. Build your family
according to the blueprints God has designed just
for you.

If you find your blueprints becoming tattered and
torn with rejection, resentment, or relapses into old

attitudes, turn on the Designer. He can build where you failed, working with and through you.

KIDS CAN KILL YOU

Every baby is born beautiful, but it doesn't take long before he becomes a battle as well as a beauty.

The outcome of every battle with a kid is determined by your intake of truth and understanding, and by your willingness to stop and listen. In the heat of battle, it is neither necessary nor prudent to show your child how Phillips, Moffat, or Taylor translates Bible verses on obedience to parents. This is show-time; you are on stage. The question is, What translation are you **showing**, not What translation are you **reading?**

Many overconfident parents think they have the answers when the kids aren't even asking any questions. Our kids don't need to be badgered with precious promises as much as they need the availability of some precious parents.

Kids see better than they hear. Parents' behavior communicates a great deal more than anything they could possibly say.

If your kid is giving you fits, find out how he sees **you**. Maybe your sound is good, but the video doesn't match. Remember, the pattern your kid most likely will copy is the one he sees at home.

The curtain is up, Mom and Dad! Do you know your parts in the dramas of your children? Keep your eyes on Jesus Christ, your Director. Your kid will come out of the show happy and mature if he knows the actors are real.

CALL YOUR KIDS

Perhaps your children are now married and living in their own home with responsibilities of their own. Maybe it has been a long time since you had a long-distance talk with those you love. Pick up that telephone and call them today. A phone call, like a personal visit, can heal years of misunderstanding.

Remember, your best friend could be your own child. And touch can prevent or heal an ouch.

It's not the big battles that win the war. The little gains and losses each day decide the outcome of any conflict.

DIVORCE IS AN OUCH!

Divorce, though never desirable, can be a time of growing or groaning. Only you can decide what will hurt you, and only you can decide how long a thing will hurt.

Divorce is a terrible experience. It is easier to bury someone than to divorce him or her. Death is complete and final. Divorce hangs on for years, always interfering with the new life, new friends, or new plans.

I hope you never suffer divorce. But if you do, you must decide to use it and not let it abuse you. Divorce can be the end of the world for you, if you let it.

But, with God's help, you can grow even through divorce. You can find new strength for the deepest hurts. You can rediscover or revamp your self-image. You can experience spiritual, emotional, or psychological renovation.

Do you feel rejected? God was rejected too, and he understands. God is in the business of making new beginnings and new people. Bring him your brokenness; he will remake you.

Dare to believe that you can go on, rebuild your dreams (in fact, dream bigger dreams than ever), do the things you always wanted to do, become the person you wanted to become.

Because you are free in the Spirit, go and sin no more. Walk into your new world, your new image, and your new freedom.

No failure is final unless you believe it so. The greatest pain in the delivery of a child is just before birth. How do you know something good is not about to be born out of your deepest sufferings?

Don't let divorce-ouch make you a grouch. An ounce of growth is better than a ton of grouch. No crisis is more than God can handle in your life.

SEX IS SENSATIONAL

Sex is unparalleled pleasure for a man and wife.

Sex is a little vacation for two from the pressures of the day.

Sex is getting lost in the presence of your mate.

Sex is forgetting what **not** to do! Two people who know how to enjoy each other will also know how to work side by side. The harder you work together, the better you understand each other intimately. Sex is a mysterious, sensational secret shared between two people who welcome the joy of working together.

You are a poor marriage partner if you refuse to walk with your spouse through the battles of life. The bedroom cannot make up for the cost of lost battles. Be victors together, and you will enjoy the triumph of the pleasure of sex.

Take time for a short vacation. The stimulation of proper sex could be the stimulant needed to lift you from defeat. Pleasure here could be power out there. Don't risk losing the romance of the bedroom. If chaos sets in here, it creates confusion on the other side of the door as well. What happens behind closed doors could determine what doors will open for you and your family.

THE WOMAN WHO OUTRUNS HER HUSBAND RUNS OUT OF HUSBANDS

The liberated woman is free—free from the very things she needs. Her liberty will win her everything she doesn't really want.

The surest route to the divorce court is for a wife to become totally independent of her husband because she is so effective in meeting all of her own needs. The "too-successful" woman who becomes involved outside the home becomes unnecessary to her husband. Her very success in the world brings her failure at home.

The woman who outruns her husband will soon run out of husbands. Such an error will bring ruin to a special relationship. When a wife shows her husband up, it isn't long before he doesn't show up.

The "liberated woman" is free.

1. She is free from being a mother to her children. (The children now have adopted mothers called baby-sitters.)
2. She is free from her husband's provision. She no longer needs him, because she cares for herself.
3. She is free from the input and leadership of the male, and all her ideas may be unbalanced in life's relationships because of this.
4. She is free to be alone and lonely. She has been liberated to her own desolation.

A woman who understands her true womanhood knows none can excel her. She controls the world, her own world, by the secret powers possessed only by a true woman. She is free to become what God made her to be—a woman of God.

LIFE STARTS IN CHAOS

God evidently created the earth "without form, and void" (Genesis 1:2, KJV). Creators and artists do not choose a perfect world in which to work. They take the underdeveloped and untried and seek to create something better and more rewarding. Out of chaos, God began to develop cosmos.

The young wife, beautiful and well-shaped, loved only by her husband, sacrifices much of her liberty to bring another human into the world. In a sense both husband and wife have to die so they can blend their two lives into a third.

Fullness of life often seems to start in chaos. You discover the meaning of living as you begin to grasp the meaning of losing. Life and death, complementing each other, make up one cycle. One dies that another may live.

The most popular stories are told by people who started at the bottom. Not many enjoy hearing about inherited success. Nehemiah rebuilt the walls of Jerusalem out of the rubbish of destruction. Walls are always more beautiful and admired, when they are reconstructed from ruins.

Learn to start where you are. If you are in chaos, take courage. You and God are on the verge of creating something new.

S I X
Create or Stagnate

Conformity does not often lead to transformation, and it is impossible to be an original conformist! If you want newness of life, don't depend too much on others. As you are true to yourself, people and ideas will offer to help you fulfill both yourself and them. Aid will come as you are engaged in the conflict of winning.

CONFORMITY CAN CRIPPLE YOU

Conformity will take you captive if you let it.

Conformity says, "Stay in line. Don't think for yourself. Do it as it has always been done." Conformity stifles creativity; creativity threatens conformity. They are ever enemies.

When too many things are alike too much of the time, variety and even discernment are endangered species. If the policies of an organization interfere with the productivity, creativity, or well-being of its people, then those policies need to be adjusted to maximize the potential development of the workers.

Likewise, dogmatism, ideological conformity, is a threat to creativity.

In some ways, you will have to conform in order to live in this world. But you also need to expand, grow, and seek new ways to escape the death trap of conformity. Finding a better way may take you to the end of the line, because not everyone wants a better way. People usually want the old way, which is all **they** know and in which **they** feel safe. But old and tried only **seems** safer.

Every new idea, concept, or procedure threatens the status quo, and so is usually rejected. This is the reason most people cling tenaciously to their old ways. I am not saying that the old is bad, or that conformity is always wrong. But once you seek to create something out of the old, be prepared to be tested and for your new ideas and new concepts to be threatened. Once you understand this, the hindrances will not catch you by surprise.

The world will buy you if it can. The church will sidestep you if possible. The threatened will bully you if you let them, being afraid of your creativity. If you succeed as a creator, you must have deep courage and solid convictions.

As Rollo May says, "It takes courage to create." He adds, "Dogmatists of all kinds—scientific, economic, moral, as well as political—are threatened by the creative freedom of the creator."

Create! Creativity builds character and just might build the kind of world your critics are looking for.

DO YOU REALLY NEED THEIR APPROVAL?

So what if you are not accepted by some people?

Many times you probably have based your worth on being accepted by one or two individuals whom you consider important.

Have you ever realized that their acceptance does not have to make that much difference in your job or your success? Many spend a lifetime hoping some particular person or special group will accept them. Usually you will discover after being accepted that it didn't make all that much difference anyway in either your person or your performance.

Too much acceptance or approval can remove the need to prove yourself. Having not to prove, you fail to improve, and thus "die." What does it really matter if "they" do not recognize or accept your efforts? Does that negate or remove your good talents? What if you are never "in"? Does that prove anything? What does being accepted or rejected really have to do with who you are or the abilities God has given you?

What upsets you indicates your level of developed character. **Who** upsets you reveals your growth in understanding. The bigger the situation has to be to bother you, the more mature you have become in Christ.

Do you think the ocean cares if a swimmer rejects the waves? Be careful how much value you put on the swimmers in your "ocean." Take a long look at the people or groups who are rejecting you. Is the effort it would take to win their approval worth being accepted by them after all?

Seeking to win approval prior to success is like seeking applause before you appear on stage. If you wait for applause before your cause is just or established, you'll miss the winner's banquet!

The only persons who must approve you for doing your best are you and God. "To thine own self be true" is more than classic Greek philosophy. It's a fact of life!

BE TRUE TO YOU

Being true to you is not self-centeredness. It's being safe!

It may take you years to come to a full understanding of how to be yourself, how to be true to your vision, how to stand independent.

A thousand voices will call you. They will tell you to change, to quit doing what you're doing, and to take up their cause (which they feel is always **the** best). But you must know who **you** are and what you are, as well as what you are doing for God. Your cause is as good or as important as the next. But if you don't have a strong conviction of this, you will rush to support and follow every flag or cause that comes your way looking for help.

Thank God for what others are doing, but thank God also for what **you** are doing. It may not seem as glamourous, but it is probably just as good. If you have any capacity for accomplishment, everyone will want to use it for their ends. Guard your influence. It is the greatest stock you have.

Do not give yourself away needlessly in order to

gain the respect or appreciation of others. Be you, and let them be them!

Dare to say to yourself, "I will not seek to make others like me. Let others accept me for what I am. And if that doesn't satisfy them, so be it. I will no longer expect others to take me where I can take myself."

This conviction will strengthen you so you can strengthen them.

There comes a time when a person must make himself worthy to succeed, and he will not lose that sense of worth even if the whole world were to forget him. He can be content with his life before God because he showed others a foundation to build on for eternity.

Only One could say, "Remember me," because he forgot no one. He, our foundation, will not abandon us.

Being true to you makes you superior to your outer world, for you will not be true to yourself and false to others. True superiority is not complex, but is the result of sincerity. Place does not prove the superiority of the person; sincerity and integrity do.

Being true to you means you are true to your God-given dreams, your desires before him, your prayers. What you really want is what you really are. Reach out for them. This is being true to you.

WHEN THERE IS NONE TO HELP—WHAT THEN?

There have been times when I've felt disappointment from being let down by a friend, misunderstood by my wife, or forsaken by people I trusted. In my hurt I looked for someone to help me, but found none. It seemed others had their own hurts, letdowns, and misunderstandings. In those dark, depressing days, I learned to stand alone, but not really alone. "The Lord stood beside Paul" (Acts 23:11).

And as God helped me, my aid became others' answers. I had "medicine" to use at the outstation clinics in life's jungle of bumped-up people, help for people engaged in the bumps and battles of living.

Where do you look when there is none to help?

You have looked to others for help, only to find them looking to you for help—two starving people trying to feed one another!

Have you found your true place of encouragement, acceptance, and power? Are you still looking to institutions, organizations, and political influence to do for you what only God can do?

All these powers will demand **from** you if they give **to** you. They will own you after they have helped you. Whoever supplies your need is your master. That's why Paul said, "[God] . . . will supply all your needs" (Philippians 4:19).

David said, "My help is from Jehovah who made the mountains" (Psalm 121:2). He had experienced the dread of looking to Saul. He had looked to his children too, only to have his favorite son betray him for the throne.

Jesus never looked to anyone but the Father. This is not to say others cannot help you. They do and will. But truly you only continue with his help. God works through people as he moves them to help you. Help may come through total strangers; it may come from people near or far. But behind it all, God is working for your good.

God fed the prophet Elijah from the mouths of ravens. He fed him from the hand of a widow, who was also a stranger.

God will also provide for you. Look to him. The Bible says, "Seek ye first the kingdom of God, and his righteousness; and all these things [clothing and food] shall be added unto you" (Matthew 6:33, KJV).

But looking for aid before you enter the battle is like looking for a hospital before you are hurt. Move ahead; God will take care of you.

THE DARK MIND DEFEATS

A darkened mind is difficult to change, challenge, or control. Once it is darkened by fears, limitations, or restrictions, it becomes almost impossible to alter. This can be done, but not at a bargain-counter price.

You will sometimes be surrounded by people who are controlled by the deep, dark feelings of their minds. They may be motivated by fear, or perhaps by limitations or traditions. To the darkened mind, the world is a fearsome place in which to live, move, and create.

Such a mind sees obstacles better than opportunities. It sees shadows as being real. It is on guard every moment against change or challenge.

The dark mind reminds me of animals that prefer the hidden crevices of the earth to the sunlight. They do not come out of hiding boldly like a lion, but retreat to avoid being hurt.

The Bible says, "The godly are bold as lions"

(Proverbs 28:1). Boldness comes from inner knowledge. It is the result of knowing who we are and who our God is.

The dark mind, unable to stand alone, seeks the company of the fearful. There is a feeling of safety in dark holes. Fearful animals run together, and the togetherness of darkness gives them strength.

The dark mind cannot tolerate being in the minority. If the minority is opposed or rejected because of a new idea or concept, little, dark-minded people will run under the umbrella of the majority and cry, "We are safe." Approval is vital to them, whether what they approve is good or bad. The dark-minded only want safety.

The Bible says, "Quit the evil deeds of darkness" (Romans 13:12). Renounce darkness in your mind today, and you may change your world tomorrow.

ECHOES ARE SELDOM REFRESHING

I hear an echo—my voice telling me what I already know! It is repeating, not creating. And the repetition ruins the original.

Seldom refreshing and never revealing, the echo serves only one purpose: it tells me I'm alone!

Go beyond the echo and learn to share whatever God has taught you about himself. Paul called the message he preached, "my gospel." In a sense the message you share, the understanding you have, or the experience you possess is yours. It becomes your gospel. The good news, as you experience it and understand it, will become good news to others as well.

The nature of God is more beautifully seen as

each one of us teaches what God has taught us about himself. There is only one God, one Person supreme in the universe. But there are many sides to God. Tell me what you know about him; then permit me to tell you what I have learned. And don't reject me just because my concept differs a little from yours.

One person may have been blind, but now he sees. Another was lost and now is found. Yet another was dead and is alive again. All experience the power of God, but the same power shines upon us in different ways.

Don't fight someone else who has a story to tell and loves to tell it. Let each one tell you how he or she met God. You'll be richer for doing so.

If you have an echo, let it go out as truth. It will come back the same, for an echo always repeats what it hears.

The more you understand what you're sending out, the greater will be your joy when it comes back.

DON'T DEPEND TOO MUCH ON OTHERS

When you depend too much on others for joy, success, or direction, you will fail to develop your own powers. Seeking the approval of others can lead to a habit of slavish dependence.

Continually looking for others to stimulate you will stymie you. You will become a victim to everyone's words, looks or actions. God is not building a victim, but a victor.

As you grow to depend on the stimuli within yourself, there will be less chance for you to stumble or be held in bondage by others.

Circumstances must not become your course. If a situation has you in its grasp, there is no possibility for you to change it. Dependence upon others for their approval or acceptance then controls you. The real you cannot come out for fear you may not be accepted. You fear your own words, actions, and suggestions, because you have entrusted your future joys to the hands of others. Being overanxious for others' stamp of approval on you and your world will threaten your potential.

Rather, know you are right with God, yourself, and the human race—then act!

If another hesitates to approve you, make sure you really need and want that approval. Is it that important to you? Is it vitally important to you? Seeming **need** can become a **weed** which chokes the **seed** of your self-acceptance if you're not careful.

If it becomes clearly impossible to receive the approval or acceptance of another, then it's no longer important to you. You don't need it. You are accepted in the Beloved.

ORIGINALS ARE USUALLY REJECTED—AT FIRST

You may sometimes have the longing thought, "If there were just another person to help me. Who will give me the spark to go on?" You may be tempted to look for outside stimulation and motivation to move you on to your dreams.

Your hopes seem slow in coming. Even worse, people tell you that your dreams will never become reality.

You stand alone. No one cares to motivate you to your destination. Some pity you; others punish you for daring to hope. The world seems to be an unfriendly battlefield as you try to blossom into your fullest potential. You are misunderstood and misrepresented. And yet, you are an **original!**

Keep in mind that originals are questioned, suspected, and usually rejected at first.

It will take years to prove your value. You have no guarantee that you will live to see the full proof of your work, or worth. It is crucial that you commit your life fully to God's care.

There is, of course, an easier way, an easier life.

1. It goes along with the norm, the accepted.
2. It never thinks for itself or seeks a better way to do anything.
3. It maintains peace by doing little.

The easy life has many compromises but few adventures.

1. It lives and dies as it is—no worse and no better.
2. It exists, keeps to itself, and moves only from known to unknown.

How much better it is to create what you must than to be crushed by a crowd of cowards.

Originals are priceless! Being one of a kind could bring you great reward now—and even more so later.

SEVEN

When Things Don't Work Out —Work On

Working on when things don't work out always works in your interest. What you are truly interested in, you will put effort into. Waiting is hard, and performing is harder; but let nothing make you retreat from the pursuit of your hopes. As long as you have hope to work on, things will work out—in time.

Someone once commented, "I believe it is better to be frustrated or even to fail in the pursuit of an idea or principle in which one deeply believes than to seek the false security of a safe and easy course through life."

If you believe in what you're doing, pursue it in the face of possible or even imminent failure. In fact, there is no way to do anything without the possibility of failure. Overcoming failure or outrunning losses is the secret of success. There never will be a time in your life when you will not be on the edge of a possible loss.

It is always better to pursue a high ideal or a

worthy goal and be constantly frustrated than to take a path of ease and false security. Only the brave see the frontiers, and they walk into them. Pioneers have tough faith. Whether facing obstacles in science or evangelism or wherever, they are touching the untouchable and enjoying the pleasure of new accomplishment.

You will find the "unlimited you" only as you seek to unlock the doors of your soul and mind. Whoever keeps you in bondage "for your own good" is your enemy. Liberty within law is the answer. Pick up your ideas and ideals again, and again, and again. Work with them. The realization that you have failed could be the beginning of your greatest success.

IS IT WORTH YOUR EFFORT?

Do you have the persistence and patience to work your way through problems that stand between you and your desired goals? My ambitious son, active in real estate, has told me, "Never set a goal unless you're willing to pay a price equal to the value of that goal." He went on to say, "If you're not willing to pay the price, it will crush your spirit and damage your self-image. The other goals you have set will be less enjoyable or perhaps neglected altogether, because you did not pay the price to reach your ultimate goal."

Set realistic, reachable goals, so you will have the ability and energy to reach them. Each goal you reach inspires you to greater heights, but woe to you if you develop a habit of stopping short of your goals.

There will always be problems standing between

WHERE THERE'S A WALL, THERE'S A WAY

you and your desired destination. You will need persistence and patience to keep pressing on until you fulfill your dreams. What price are you willing to pay? How long will you pursue the goal? Is it worth your effort? What will happen to your family, or to your spiritual or physical powers while working through the problems between you and your destination? All of these things must be weighed in light of the value and worth of your objective.

If you do accomplish your goal, what will the rewards be for you, your world, or God? Settle these questions, and the rest will follow easily. Your effort will intensify as your interest in your goals grows. The involvement of going on is equal to your interest in the objective. Only you know what captures your interest and what you really want to do with your life.

WHAT WILL IT TAKE TO SEND YOU BACK?

How long will you strive toward your dreams, goals, hopes, and prayers? What would it take to send you back from these life-changing aspirations?

Have you ever thought about Joshua and Caleb and how long they kept at it until they crossed the Jordan River and so gained the Promised Land? They walked with defeatists and complainers for forty years!

All twelve spies had seen the land. It was beyond description, with excellent fruit that was theirs for the taking. But the whole nation turned back in less than thirty days to wander in the hot sands, hoping for a better day. They could have taken what was theirs, their special gift from God, but they did not believe in themselves and their ability to take the land. They agreed to accept defeat without an effort. They gave up the battle before the bugle called for war. And it all seemed so right!

They waited in vain for a better day to come. But the day never came—for them.

In contrast, Joshua and Caleb kept the faith. These two men kept their eyes on the Promised Land as the years rolled by. The defeaters passed away (they usually do). Finally the day came to cross the Jordan and claim the inheritance. Perseverance led to the reality of true success.

The battles were not easy; the going was tough in the new land. But these two men had been toughened by all the delay and were ready to throw all they had into the attempt to take the land. And, with God's help, they took it! All of it!

How long will you keep at it? What could send you back? To succeed, you must be willing to keep going even if the whole world turns back, leaving you alone in your quest.

Hold firmly to your hope, keep trusting God, and one day hope will give way to sight. How long you keep at it will be determined by how long you are satisfied to live in the defeated camp. Let your dissatisfaction become inspirational, and you will take the "land" today.

THE WAITING ROOM IS HARD

When things don't work out—wait on! There is a time for working, and there is a time for waiting. You can grow through waiting.

Corrie ten Boom once said with a sigh, "Waiting is the hardest thing I ever do." In this age of instant products, people want instant answers to prayer, instant maturity in grace, and instant success without having to wait.

Noah waited 120 years for the promised rain, having never seen rain before.

Abraham was 100 years old before he finally received the promised son, Isaac.

Joseph sat in prison, a reject, for fourteen years, waiting for God's plan to unfold.

Waiting is part of receiving.

Being sent to the waiting room is hard. Time crawls there, and an hour seems like eternity. No one enjoys a vigil in the waiting room. But you grow through waiting.

You grow while waiting for a baby to be born.

You grow while waiting for school days to end.

You grow while waiting for the tide to change.

Growing is a natural process of groans, goals, and God-likeness. God uses waiting to help us grow.

It is never easy to accept delays, denials, or defeats. But these are part of life. Welcome the waiting times, or at least accept them. Use your delays. Sharpen your talents, enlarge your plans, and strengthen your hopes while you wait.

The silence of the waiting room is stifling. But in the silence there is a sacred Presence. His name is God, and he is a God of hope.

SOLITUDE IS SACRED

In this age of noise and clatter, it pays to learn the joys of silence. Turn off the radio or TV; ignore the telephone. Listen! You just might hear God's voice telling you how to win over your struggles.

There's a balance between silence and sound which you must learn if you are to discover how to get to where you ought to be going. Knowing when to speak up and when to shut up is a science. Writers and public speakers understand this. Wise people practice it.

All creative people testify to classic clues coming to them through solitude. Your speaking up can be more effective after you have learned the secrets of shutting up. Showing up in history is sometimes a matter of knowing when to speak up.

Moses learned this on the mount. What he heard there, he spoke in the valley.

Jesus knew this powerful secret also. He spent much of his time in solitude. But when he spoke, it was unlike any other man who ever spoke.

There will be times when you must not speak if you are to hear. Sometimes, if you are to see, you must close your eyes. The secrets of the universe are found in silence. It is often the "still, small voice" that reveals the mind of God.

Solitude is sacred. To the learner, coming out of the silence will be like unlocking the cage of the tiger. Freedom means more when it has been temporarily restricted and self-imposed. The disciples coming from their Pentecost waiting room turned the world upside-down. Things have never been the same since then and never will be again.

"Stand silent! Know that I am God!" (Psalm 46:10). These are words of power to be heeded.

The next time you feel dull, fearful, or inadequate, try keeping quiet. Perhaps the next time you speak, the world will listen. Performance is perfected in the privacy of your heart, and what you see there will be flashed to the world.

THE SECRET OF PERFORMING

Performance is a product of knowing who you are.

Furthermore, you will never work on unless you know **what** you're working on.

Motivation depends on knowledge. You cannot do something well if you are unsure it's a wise thing for you to do.

Performance comes from knowing that what you are doing is right. You will always do well if you know the correct way to do a thing and are persuaded it is right for you. On the flipside, people practice evil because they convince themselves evil is prudent.

Many people are not busy, motivated, or interested in what they're doing because they aren't sure whether their involvements are really right for them. "Is this the direction I should go? Is this the best way to do what I'm doing?" Questions like these curtail productivity.

Thomas asked Jesus the way to heaven. Jesus answered, "I am the way (John 14:6, KJV). Thomas was willing to make a start, but he needed to know the direction. John said, "We do know that we know him" (1 John 2:3). This is not boasting. Being sure we have found God's direction for us is basic to all progress and security.

WORK ON YOUR ANXIETIES

Learning to control your anxieties is crucial, for anxiety leads to overindulgence regarding the natural appetities of the body. When I am plagued by anxiety, I eat, eat, eat. Some people sleep. Others spend money foolishly, or fall into gloom, depression, or criticism.

Uncontrolled anxiety will put on fat and take off prosperity. When your anxiety runs wild, there isn't enough money, pleasure, or people in the entire world to bring you peace.

Unhappy people are usually overindulgent in one area in life. Those who are overindulgent in more than one area are to be pitied.

Out-of-control people have lost their contentment. "Godliness with contentment is great gain," we are told in the Bible (1 Timothy 6:6, KJV). Contentment and control walk together.

Lack of contentment spoils all the good you have gathered around you. None of it will satisfy you.

Also, the contented can live on less. The little things in life will fulfill them.

1. They enjoy a cup of tea on Sunday afternoon.
2. They find joy in a baby's face.
3. They delight in a dog's bark.
4. They enjoy a grandmother's wrinkled face.

Nothing is too little or too insignificant to the contented.

Learn to control your anxieties. Don't misunderstand—you will have anxiety, plenty of it; but the secret is to control it. If this is accomplished, many of your woes will pass—in time. The Bible says, "Don't worry about anything; instead, pray about everything" (Philippians 4:6). Anxiety is the result of:

1. looking at your faults.
2. rejecting your place in the world.
3. comparing yourself with others.
4. being fearful of your future.
5. wondering what others think.

Cast your anxiety on the Lord. "Let him have all your worries and cares, for he is always thinking about you and watching everything that concerns you" (1 Peter 5:7).

Do your best with what you have where you are, with the Lord's help.

MAKE YOUR DECISIONS RIGHT ONES

Everyone says, "Make right decisions." But the winners in life go a step further, making the decisions that they do make right. I may not always make right decisions, but if I'll pay the price, I can make most of them right in time.

Always make your decisions to be right for you. **You,** seeking God's guidance, must decide what is right.

Winning in life is not easy, but it can be done. If you make 51 percent of your decisions correctly, you are over the top. You can't always be right, but you can always aim for it. Aim to hit the bull's-eye, but don't wait until all things point to just the right choice. There will be times when you must decide something, trusting God to make up the difference if you choose wrongly. No one will discern God's guidance perfectly at all times.

Trust God's providence. Trust his timing, and trust your talents. Trust other people too, but not gullibly.

God uses many ways to show you where to go and how to get there.

You are sometimes forced to make decisions in the face of problems, people, and pressures; never refuse to make decisions because of these factors. No matter what problem confronts you, make your decision. Problems, people, and pressures are not as important as the correct decision.

Everybody benefits when a right decision is made. The New Testament says, "It seemed good to the Holy Spirit and to us . . ." (Acts 15:28). Here is the secret and security of all decision: seek God's mind and make your move.

What if you make a mistake? What if a wrong decision brings your progress to a halt? Simply decide to correct whatever needs to be corrected. Such correction could solve the problem before you. Remember: a wrong decision corrected is as good as a right decision, and can yield just as much benefit.

E I G H T
Pessimism Pulverizes!

Pessimism pulverizes potential.

When you let a pessimistic attitude set up shop in your life, the roses fade, the sunset is darkened, and the stars are silent. Nothing gets through to your heart if pessimism prevails.

The disciples once stood before 5,000 hungry people with practically no money to buy food. Their only resources were the five loaves and two fishes offered by a little boy. "But what good is that with all this mob?" they questioned (John 6:9). The limitations of the situation had eclipsed their potential in Jesus.

There are religious pessimists, social pessimists, economic pessimists, matrimonial pessimists, emotional pessimists.

They all say nothing is good, nobody is right, the church is gone, money is tight, homes and marriages are finished, the government is communistic, the devil has won.

There are "limited pessimists" also. They say nothing is ever enough; everything is about to run out.

Pessimism dampens the spirit, destroys hope, and distorts the truth. Nothing is quite right when one's attitude is pessimistic. Any degree of progress is unrecognized by a pessimist.

Helen Keller said, "Nothing great is ever accomplished in a spirit or atmosphere of pessimism because the pessimist has already concluded that nothing can be done to change a disagreeable situation."

Why are you pessimistic? Think about it.

You can overcome this attitude by recounting your assets, giving praise to God for what you do have, and doing what you can to change your situation for the better. Everything can change, if **you** are willing to change.

Don't let anything pulverize **your** potential.

HOW TO MAKE YOURSELF MISERABLE

It is really quite simple. Start by thinking about your failures. This will get the ball rolling.

The truth is, only **you** can make yourself miserable. In fact, you can train yourself so that you will "enjoy" your miseries daily. But it takes time and effort to learn the trade, and you will never know unlimited misery unless you are determined to achieve it.

Think about your failures each day. Make sure you don't forget one. Tell yourself it's important to remember others' unkind remarks about your job, your home, or your family. Recounting the fears and losses you have been through will pay incredible dividends.

Remember that people enjoy hearing about your hurts and disappointments. The best way to impress people and strangers is to talk about all of your troubles in the most minute detail. Go as far as you can into the past and move on to the present, relating all the many ways you have failed.

Whatever you do, confess **all** your marital conflicts to your children and to the people at prayer meeting. This will help them feel as miserable as you do. Thus, your problems will become their prayer concern. In this way everyone will be thinking of you and your desperate need for much more love and understanding.

Besides these basic requirements for "miserability," remember never to pay your bills on time. Let the bank, creditors, and the church wait thirty days (or more) after payment is due. This will remind them that you are independent of their help and will make them love you and fear you even more.

Whatever you do, don't let God run your life—he could ruin it. Holding back on him will guarantee you the joy of being miserable every day.

Good luck!

HOW TO MAKE ENEMIES

In this same vein, let me show you how to effectively hinder the "unlimited you" when meeting people. It takes a powerful self-image to turn friends into enemies, but it can be done if you try.

For example, when you meet a person for the first time, be sure to mispronounce his name and to tell him you thought he was somebody else.

Hasten to tell him all of your success stories first, before he can tell you his. Let him know he is talking to a winner. He will long remember you for your sense of humor and outstanding abilities.

Another important tactic in making an enemy is to tell him how spiritually minded you are. Remind him how many prayers you have had answered, and so give him the impression that you have an "in" with God. Be sure he understands that few people ever get **that** close to God!

You might also stress the fact that you are in the apostolic line—Paul didn't have anything on you. This will put him in awe of your religious concepts and spiritual importance. No doubt he will call you first the next time he needs prayer.

Also, as you court rejection, apologize repeatedly for being his friend and never include him in your success. Always be wishy-washy in making your decisions too. And if you want to really be rejected, be critical of his other friends. This should do it.

This is the kind of pessimism which pulverizes. Keep trying, and you—yes, you—can be the most miserable person on the block.

GETTING FAT TAKES WORK

Remember, the "unlimited you" cannot be hindered by being fat. Don't let anybody tell you that overweight people are not loved.

Getting fat takes a lot of work, though. You will have to reach for the refrigerator door each time you pass it. It takes a lot of energy to carry the food to your favorite place, jogging to the kitchen for refills, and jogging back to your favorite chair, but keep at it.

Jogging from the front room to the kitchen is good for your heart. Don't mind the food you are consuming; just keep telling yourself that jogging from TV room to kitchen and back will cause you to lose it.

Keep in mind that fat people look prosperous. Obesity or even slight overweight proves you have money to buy what you like to eat. In fact, it proves you have both the time and the money to get fat.

Also remember that fat people have more fun, and they don't have to live as long as other people in this troubled world. The fatter you are, the sooner you will leave your problems behind. That should make you happy.

Remind yourself too that there are worse sins than overeating. Compare yourself to the drunkard, and compliment yourself for not being in **his** category.

Tell yourself that others should lose weight, but not you. Impress in your mind that your weight looks better on you than it does on anybody else.

Whatever you do, promise yourself that someday you will lose a few pounds—when you reach thirty, or forty, or . . .

Now I will share some other ways you can learn to be miserable. You can pulverize anything if you try.

NEGATIVISM GETS WHAT YOU DON'T WANT

You have the potential for unlimited negative thinking if you choose it and use it wisely. Negative thinking and a negative attitude will get you everything you don't want. You will have to fight off all the positive books, positive sermons, and positive people to develop this strong, negative attitude. But it can be done if you are determined to be miserable.

The power of negative thinking can even help you lose your job. Always come to work with the thought in mind that you deserve a better place to work. Make sure you bring the boss all your problems. (After all, he **is** the boss and wants to know all the complaints, lack of money, and any general unrest that exists among the workers in your department.) If you come often enough with problems and difficulties, he will reward you with a pink slip. Having solved your problems, he will have no further need for you. This is one of the great benefits of negative thinking.

The power of negative thinking will inspire you to find a job worthy of your talents, intelligence, and self-made powers. When you apply for the job, let the boss know he would be lucky to have you on the team. Tell him how you corrected your past bosses regarding their failure to recognize and understand your abilities. Impress him with the fact that you are always willing to take less money if promotions are automatic—you are anxious for the top.

If these things don't put you in the ranks of the unemployed, try the following: (1) Always come in a little late. This shows you are independent. (2) Leave the job a little early, to beat the traffic. You can save energy this way by going ahead of the traffic. Let the boss know you left early in order to save energy on the light bill. Surely he will appreciate your loyalty to the energy crisis. (3) Whatever you do, don't overwork. It could jeopardize the other workers in your office.

You have unlimited power to get everything in life you don't want. Use it or lose it.

Now let's learn another lesson on pulverizing—in the home.

HOW TO RAISE CRIMINALS IN THE HOME

Let me tell you how to raise criminals. If you really want bad kids, the type that will break your heart or give you something to make you prayerful, then you must start early in the lives of your children.

You must first begin to hate them before they are born. Despise the fact that you got pregnant, wish that this baby had never been conceived, resent the fact that you have to be limited and hindered in your home and recreational activities because of this child. That's a good start in raising a criminal.

After the child is born, set out to make him the most ideal baby in the world. Tell youself, "He's going to be a perfect child in the home, the community, and especially the church." This overstrict attitude should do a lot to aid him in going astray.

The next step in raising a criminal is to give him everything he wants. Let him believe that life is fair. You may have had little or nothing as a child, but don't let this happen to your youngster. Never let him earn money in the home. Remind him that the home is not a place where you earn your allowance—it is free. Impress on him that the whole world owes him a living.

If these don't work, threaten him with divorce.

Don't let him feel secure in the love between Mom and Dad. This should build insecurity deep within his personality and shake him loose from any kind of stability.

The final suggestion in raising a criminal is, never tell him God loves him. Never let him know he's special. Point out all his weaknesses and failures, and at the same time impress on him the fact that if he does it again he will be disliked and rejected by you. This should do the trick.

Are you learning to pulverize?

HOW TO DEFEAT OPPORTUNITY

You can defeat every good opportunity if you try.

First, don't take advantage of opportunities—they could turn sour. Let no one talk you into taking a risk for any reason. Make sure everything you do is safe, secure, and sure to succeed before you step through the door on which opportunity is knocking.

You must always keep in mind that the pure, honest person will never succeed in this world. This world is not made for saints but for sinners.

Remind yourself often that it is not godly to succeed. Tell yourself that God's greatest people are plagued with problems and sorrows. You can defeat every opportunity.

You can defeat your marriage too, by telling yourself: (1) I should have married another person, or (2) I got married too soon (or if that doesn't work, I got married too late). But the final blow in defeating opportunities for happiness in your marriage is to tell your partner: (3) you made a mistake.

You also can defeat your vocation or career. Make

sure you keep a humble attitude by daily telling yourself you are unworthy of job joys and especially the raise in pay you received for your inferior work.

Always keep your weaknesses before you. Tell yourself and those you work with that you don't do your job well or never had the right training for it. They will probably tell the boss and you will get an open door—to the outside.

You can defeat your faith as well, if you try. Make sure you hear clearly, fully, and comprehensively all the gossip about your church and its leaders. This will sustain your ability to defeat opportunities for fellowship and growth. Don't trust the church with your money. Give your money somewhere else where people don't know you personally.

Above all else, you can defeat your faith if you don't bother to pray and trust God. Trusting God could lead you into a trap; prayer could cause you to change the false image you have of yourself.

You can defeat every opportunity if you try, but it will take effort on your part.

Enjoy your misery!

DEPRESSION DEADENS

Enough of this ridiculous negativism! Let's get serious again.

Seek to be as happy as possible in your situation. Happiness heals and is a light in the darkness. Determine to be happy with the home you have, the job you hold, and the present situation you are in. This is not to say you must remain as you are, but it is saying you will not change your situation unless you have peace in it. Only happy hearts are free to expand or to effect change.

Depression deadens. The horizon always looks dark to the defeated heart.

Begin to be happy where you are. Make sure you have seen all the areas of your life that are good (it can't be **all** bad). Find the things that thrill your heart. Be careful not to let the negative and distasteful overshadow the hopeful.

There are many people who feel "good" only when they feel bad. They prefer the dark side of life. Their eyes have been trained to see better in the dark. When the world falls apart, they feel some sort of comfort. This is sick thinking. The healing power of happiness can expel this dark demon of gloom.

Jesus used the word "blessed" for "happiness." He had much to say about peace, joy, happiness, and the abundant life. But happiness must not end with **you** if you want to continue to be happy. You are happy in order to share it with others. Usually happy people are sharing people; they are channels. Give away happiness, and you will build it in your own life.

Be happy where you are. This alone can take you where you want to go.

N I N E
What You See, Sees You

What you see determines what you want to see!

Your fruit reflects your roots!

The good things in life do not "drop in" if you have "dropped out."

All pleasure is the result of preparation and perspiration.

Your future is fixed by the faithfulness of the moment.

Let's see how all these things can work for you and not against you.

WHAT YOU SEE, SEES YOU

Here are some undeniable laws of God in his universe.

1. What captures your attention, captures your attendance.
2. Your gaze determines your direction.
3. You grow where you go.
4. The fruit represents the root.

5. What you like is what you love.
6. What you learned is what you loved.
7. What you sow is what you reap.
8. What you pay attention to, pays you.
9. The pension determines the attention.
10. Whatever you gaze at will eventually capture you.

You will only see what has your attention. The grip of the gaze determines your destiny.

The serpent's secret of survival is its power to charm. If the bird can be charmed by the serpent, it will be captured and destroyed. Similarly, whatever has your attention has you.

The only hope of breaking the spell of death for that little bird is to break the gaze. Likewise, the spell of defeat and discouragement in your life can only be broken by removing your gaze.

Glance at evil or gaze at good—the choice is yours.

Peter walked on the water when others were afraid to do so. But the second he looked at the problem of the waves, down he went. You have been taught all your life to watch out for problems, and you have always found plenty of problems to watch out for.

You will always see whatever you are looking for—good or bad, problems or potentials, trials or triumphs, sin or Christ.

Turn your attention away from the obvious to the opportune. Look away from problems to possibilities.

Think of all the reasons you can do and have the things you want. The greater your reasons, the greater will be your results.

Perseverance depends on keeping your gaze in the right direction. The Bible gives the key: "Keep your eyes on Jesus, our leader and instructor" (Hebrews 12:2).

Remember this law: What you take will in time take you over. The taking over starts in the undertaking!

DON'T WORRY ABOUT WHAT YOU MISSED

Learn to accept the fact that you will never get some things you wanted. But, on the other hand, never give up if you really want them. No doubt you will miss much in life, but you will also **have** much in life. Climbing a ladder starts at the bottom, and the bottom is not all bad. Looking up the ladder is the first step. The rest follows.

Don't worry about what you missed; just be concerned about what you have, and do something with that. A little can become much in a short time.

God will do what he can for you—if you will!

Moses never tasted the fruit of the Promised Land. He saw it, but never settled in it. Many of the prophets died without ever seeing the full realization of their hopes. The Bible says, "These men of faith . . . died without ever receiving all that God had promised them" (Hebrews 11:13).

No doubt you will see much before you die. It is better to have looked for much and gained little than to have looked for little and gained nothing.

Count the things you do see, and let these stimulate further hopes. Don't keep your mind on the things you didn't see or accomplish. Rather, gaze on what you and God can yet do.

The negative has tremendous force. If it catches you off-guard, down you'll go. Only the positive can pull you up. Use the negative to aid the positive; let it drive you to success and answers. Let the bumps teach you to install shock absorbers in your faith.

Never give up on what you want unless what you want is not what you really need!

True need keeps coming back, awakening desire. But it's desire which finally fulfills the need.

Don't worry about what you missed; maybe it wasn't worth it anyway. Capture today.

DEVELOP YOUR AWARENESS

Before each step of success, you will have an awareness or consciousness that what you want is about to happen. Consciousness of the thing desired always comes before you actually have it. Each failure is preceded by that same law as well. Either you just knew something was not going to work or you had a deep feeling it would, and your knowing helped produce the result. Your heart is the chart; follow it! The pure in heart follow its promptings.

This is the reason Jesus gave an awareness of power and authority to the disciples long before he died. He said to them, "You are the world's light . . . . You are the world's seasoning . . . . You will receive power . . . . Your strength must come from the Lord's mighty power within you . . . . I have given them . . . the glorious unity of being one, as we are" (Matthew 5:14; 5:13; Acts 1:8, Ephesians 6:10; John 17:22).

First there is awareness, then assurance that the thing desired is possible or attainable.

Always there will be that knowing before it happens. Faith sees the possibility. This is God's preparation for your protection. As you seek the kingdom of God, "he will give . . . to you" (Matthew 6:33). Why? Because the kingdom includes much more than the things you are seeking to attain.

Develop your awareness. Guard it carefully.

Keep the doors to your soul well protected by praise, faith, hope, and love.

The greater the knowing, the sooner the showing of the things you are aware of.

Hope in the spirit of hope. The dividends will equal your interest if you do. In this way you will build your world out of the things you are putting into your consciousness.

Watch your consciousness. It determines what you'll finally create.

BUILD A NEW WORLD

If you expect to reach the top, you'll have to go over the top, and this involves risk. Security and playing it safe bring about stagnation.

Reach today toward your greatest goal. Do not let limitations of any kind stop you from reaching for it. Work, imagination, and inspiration will be required, but you must try.

Why not sit down now and build in your mind the kind of world you would like to live in. Then start reaching for it.

The unlimited keeps coming to the person who knows no limits. The more you have, the more

you'll get. "For to him who has will more be given
. . . and he will have great plenty" (Matthew 13:12).

Dare to reach through your obstacles. Reach
around your hindrances. Reach over the top. Reach
under the bottom.

Teach yourself to reach! When you reach out,
things and people will reach back.

Visualize yourself in possession of the things you
are reaching for. You may be disappointed at times,
but keep reaching in confidence.

The Bible tells you, "Cheer up! Take courage if
you are depending on the Lord" (Psalm 31:24). You
need courage only if there is a possibility of defeat
or loss. It takes courage to live, to grow, to expand.

Reach for your goals today. If you don't start today,
when will you start? There is an unlimited world
waiting for you if you reach for it. The world you'd
like to build is waiting to be built.

Put God in your world. Together the two of you
will make a great construction company.

LET NOTHING STOP YOU

The highest purposes can be fulfilled by anyone.
Will it be you? God is willing. Are you?

God is not in the shortage, stopping, or stumbling
business. He started the world to run it—with you.
He put you on earth hoping you would have enough
discernment to see his hand of plenty, power, and
provision! The world is for **you**, and God is **for** you.

Nothing stops God! Walk in him, and let him work
through you. You and he can succeed in this world.
Then all your defeats or victories will be on his time

schedule. It would be easier to stop the sun from shining than to block a great purpose.

God's plans for your life will happen! They must happen! Your life is like a child about to be born, and all of nature will work to bring it to pass.

The greatest care in your life should be to make sure you are fulfilling your highest aspirations, for your hopes and dreams come from God, the great Designer, the great Mover. You are a child of God; therefore, you must be a designer and a mover as well.

If you are controlled by envy, hate, or jealousy, you can only expect defeat. Defeat can only produce defeat, but life produces life.

Clean out the festering sores in your heart. Burn up the evidence against your enemies. I did, and it freed me. You will never have the miracle you need if your heart and mind are not clean and clear. Only integrity brings prosperity.

Don't allow yourself to be overcome by the hindrances or blockades that others place before you. All achievers have had to climb over other people's obstacles to reach their goals.

If you are at fault with anyone, anywhere, say so, then let it go. Maintain as much harmony as you can with your outside world. And within your own heart, let peace reign. All success and failure is born there.

WHAT WILL YOU BE DOING AT EIGHTY-FOUR?

An eighty-four-year-old soda fountain hostess was fixing three sodas for Ruth Ann, Howard Olson, and myself. She still ran her own little drugstore in the quaint country town of Hudson, Iowa. Kids from the local school often dropped by for an ice cream cone, a soda, or simply to look around for some small thing to buy.

She had just returned from Israel where she had suffered a broken hip. I thought it might be too much for her to be in a foreign country, in a strange hospital, with a fractured hip. But not this little warrior.

This little lady was bold enough to live. In a matter of a few months she was out of the hospital and back on her feet, making chocolate sodas for us and the children.

She had glued many little sayings to the napkin dispenser on the counter. Here is one of them:

Even if you are on the right track, you will get run over if you just sit there.

Try this one on for size:

To try when there is little hope is to risk failure. Not to try at all is to guarantee it.

All of her little proverbs indicated that she is a success-minded woman at eighty-four.

Happiness and success depend on your interest in life. If you lose interest in the things of life, you may be "dead" at sixteen. And interest is dependent on involvement. And involvement depends on insight. The more you know or the greater the insight, the deeper the involvement, and the happier the achievement.

What will you be doing when you are eighty-four years of age?

Faith in your future is determined by your faithfulness in the present. What you have tomorrow started yesterday.

WINTER IN THE SOUL

The temperature of the soul depends on the fuel in the heart.

You will experience darkness and coldness in your soul many times as the potential within you develops. As there is a cycle of seasons in nature, so there is a cycle of the soul.

At one moment all is light, like the burst of morning. Darkness seems to be gone forever. Scarcely a moment later, a person you meet or a situation you face casts darkness and coldness over your soul again. Don't be disheartened. This too will pass; spring is coming.

Winter in the soul is hard; delays are always difficult. At times you may think the snow will never melt from your garden of hope. But the sun always shines someplace, and your time will come. Wait and trust God.

Be sure you are ready when the light shines. It **is** coming, but are you prepared? How do you get ready for the light?

1. Be true to yourself.
2. Keep your heart pure and your motives clean.
3. Keep close to your dreams and hopes.
4. Don't let hope phase out of your life because of delay, discouragement, or destruction.

Stay in the light. Keep reminding yourself, "It will all change. It will all improve. I praise God for the delay, the trouble, and the patience to wait."

The Bible says, "Trust in the Lord . . . . Be kind and good to others" (Psalm 37:3).

While you wait, do good. Open your hand to another who waits also. Put the cloak of praise on the shoulders of someone else who sits in cold depression. By lifting another, you will lift yourself.

Some things grow in the dark; some animals survive better in the cold. But you will prosper only in God's light.

Don't give up! If you do, it could be the end.

PROBLEM-SPOTTING

Problems can indicate that you are growing.

Problems often mean you are moving ahead and will be inevitable as you develop the "unlimited you."

Prayer warriors handle big problems. Big dreamers discover big difficulties.

The struggle to survive is a sign of life. If there is no such struggle, there is no life.

When you have all the bills paid, all the foundations laid, and are too secure, your life will be meaningless unless you discover a new challenge. Security is suicide if it stifles your creativity.

If you are thinking big, you will have problems. If you are developing, you will have difficulties.

Some people never "fumble the ball" only because they are never in the game and so never even get their hands on the ball.

The next time a big problem hinders your growth, thank God for it. It's a sure sign you are alive and moving. You would not know where to improve or grow without an indicator like this.

Take inventory today. You may have just what it takes to solve the situation you now face. Move ahead **because** of your problem!

TEN

Experiencing the Excitement of Failure

Judge yourself not by your falls, but by your desire to get up. Remember, out of that failure you can gain wisdom. Your failure could be the key to all your future success! A willingness to fail in an attempt to succeed is even greater than actual success!

EVERYONE NEEDS TO EXPERIENCE FAILURE

"Dad, you never let me fail as a boy growing up," said my son. "I think everybody needs the experience of failure at least once." His statement came as a shock to me. What he was really saying was that I had never let him believe he was a failure when he failed. There is a big difference in failing (which he did many times, and I never told him) and letting him think like a failure.

You will fail every day in some way great or small. It is impossible to always say the correct word, to react to every situation smoothly and easily, or to do the proper thing in all situations. Face the fact that you're human; you sometimes fall short of your goals.

Sometimes failure will in some way be forced on you by others. Even in those times don't label yourself a "failure" or give up. Regroup and prepare for the next round in the battle of faith.

People will let you down; circumstances won't always turn out like you expected; things don't always come together. But this does not necessarily mean failure. It could be merely a delay of your dreams, a challenge to find another way. If you conclude it's all over, it is—for you. Someone else may walk the same path and triumph there because he believed in succeeding more than in failing.

Don't let another person do what you were meant to do. Don't give your place, your calling, to anyone. The Bible says, "Hold tightly to the little strength you have—so that no one will take away your crown" (Revelation 3:11). But remember—to gain a crown, you will have to carry a cross.

A lesson too seldom learned is: seeds of success are always found in failure. Someplace in your fall, in your mistake, is the key to succeeding. Once you know what you did wrong, correct it; you will then arrive safely at second base in the game of life.

NOT ALL FAILURE IS BAD

Failure does not have to defeat you. Failure can be your greatest step toward your biggest success. Failing tells you that you need more preparation, a greater understanding of God's plans for your life.

If you truly understand failure, you will see the way to success. One is a glove, the other a hand. The two go together.

No one has ever really succeeded without previously failing miserably. You could become the greatest where you have failed the deepest, if you would just believe it. The very point of failure can become your greatest accomplishment.

Success is always found near failure. Look for it. Reexamine the place where you failed, for there you will find the secret ingredient of your success.

Undoubtedly you failed at a point where you almost succeeded. Somewhere in your failure, your stumble, your misdirection, you will find the correct procedure for the fulfillment of your greatest dreams.

The most tragic failure is saying, "I almost made it!"

You can only fail where you seek to succeed. A player who drops the ball had the opportunity to make a touchdown. Don't quit the game of life because you fumbled the ball. Recognize what went wrong, then adjust to the opposition and run the play again. The very fact that you dare to run again might cause the opposition to be taken by surprise, and that surprise could be a step toward your highest success.

Not all failure is bad, but at the same time do not become complacent with defeat. If failure becomes a way of life, you will have no life to enjoy. Your potential will develop only as you seek to understand failure and use it to your advantage.

DEFEAT CAN BECOME A WAY OF LIFE

If you're not careful, you can come to love your troubles more than your triumphs. Your prison can become home to you, feeling more familiar than the pleasure of being free.

Bondage, defeat, and failure can become your personal preference, rather than victory and liberty. Someone once said, "Beware of the chains you forge in life."

On the other hand, the things which have caused you the deepest grief can become your crown. But the cross must precede the crown. Don't stop at the cross; accept the power of resurrection. Live outside the tomb.

If you do not free your mind from the pleasures of pain, you will be caught in a trap of self-pity. Yes, there **is** pleasure in suffering; there is a certain glory in being the underdog. You may hate the bondage, but you will cleave to it unless you see a greater purpose for your life. Let your suffering draw you to the healing touch of Jesus. Bring your hurt to God; then leave the rest to him.

How can you free yourself from bondage to fear, suffering, or hurt? You can't. So surrender them all to God. Let go of them. Stop talking about them. Dare to thank God for the loss or hurt and those who caused it. Your troubles will become weights which you lift by prayer and praise, thereby strengthening your spiritual and moral muscles.

SUCCESS IN FAILURE

One Easter Sunday morning the church was packed. Cars were turned away because there was no room to park. Some people parked two or more blocks from the church; others left to attend another church.

We had just installed a $30,000 sound system. The choir was ready. The music was ready. Everything was ready. The TV cameras, the ushers, and the staff were all in place.

I rose to preach, and suddenly felt like a novice who doesn't know what to say. The sermon didn't come, but the sweat sure did. There I was, facing the biggest crowd of the year, and preaching like a beginner. The words (and thoughts) just would not come.

The service finally ended, and our children took Ruth Ann and me out for Easter dinner. We had steak and all the trimmings, and everything was at its best. But I sat there like a dead man, hardly knowing what we said or ate. I had failed—or so I thought.

At the evening service some of my congregation expressed deep appreciation for that morning's sermon. I was shocked and wondered about their intelligence.

That Monday morning, at breakfast, I was still stewing. On that occasion a good friend told me, "Sometimes the sermon isn't for you, but for someone else, apart from your own feelings." He went on to say, "God allows you to struggle in order to reach another who needed to hear what you didn't know you said." I walked out of that restaurant more mature. I saw success in failure.

Less than three weeks later a young married couple sat in my office. For the past eleven months they had had much marital difficulty. But on Easter,

99

in the midst of my "failure," this couple was reunited in love. The husband said, "Sunday morning's sermon was the turning-point in my life."

Who knows what your stumbling might produce?

I had experienced the excruciating pain of failure, but less than three weeks later it turned to the excitement of failure. I suffered, but another succeeded.

LOOK FOR YOUR FORTUNES IN YOUR MISFORTUNES

You will suffer many misfortunes in your life. Even after many victories, setbacks will come your way.

All winners, all people of great potential, must pass through the fire in order to refine their gold. The greater your potential, the greater the pressures that you will face. Only the strong succeed.

All composers, writers, and creators have had losses—plenty of them. They know the sting of failure and rejection, but it is their struggles that have caused their works to be remembered. The pain of the cross becomes the power of the cross.

You **will** suffer. You will experience loss and rejection. Growing toward your unlimited self will be perceived as a threat by some, and this too will produce pressure.

Your enemies do not realize that God is using them to perfect you. They are his instruments to bring about your good.

You will never know what you can do until you are placed under pressure. Let your cross become your crown. Be like Paul, who said, "I am glad to boast about how weak I am; I am glad to be a living demonstration of Christ's power" (2 Corinthians 12:9). Turn your infirmities to insights through faith.

You will suffer misfortunes, but through them you will gain the good things God has for you.

Hidden in your misfortune is your fortune. Your mistakes could become stakes for greater growth. "Lengthen thy cords, and strengthen thy stakes" (Isaiah 54:2, KJV).

FAILING COURAGEOUSLY

There is much to be said about failing courageously. It may mean failing while seeking to find your true dream, but nevertheless expressing your true hope and attempting to build the world you feel God has intended for you to build.

One of the great secrets I learn again and again is to be true to myself. When you truly speak your heart and show forth your inner being, you will begin unlocking your potential. As long as you hide away your innermost thoughts, you are imprisoning your spirit.

Only the free spirit is creative.

Bondage is the result of not allowing yourself to be you.

Failing successfully is failing while at your best.

I have succeeded and at the same time known I had failed. When self-respect is lowered or impaired, either because you succeeded at the expense of others or because you buried your true personality, you lost. But this loss will be known only to you, and that is its danger. Something starts to erode in you, and a spark can soon become a holocaust.

Can you succeed in being you? Yes, and don't let anyone tell you differently.

If you are going to fail, then fail while making the attempt to succeed. Recognize your limitations. It's better to have a true inferiority than a complex. The first problem can be corrected by growth.

GET UP AGAIN

Paul Harvey has enthusiastically said, "Get up when you fall down." The ability to get up after you have fallen or been knocked down is the secret of every achievement.

Almost-winners are never truly satisfied. You will fall down many times. You may be knocked down by your enemies, your ignorance, or your competitors. But if you are afraid of being knocked down, you will never reach the goal line. Being knocked down, falling, is part of the game of life. You must be willing to pick yourself up again and again. No bruises—no gold medals.

Your losses may even outnumber your wins. But keep at it and you will finally be a winner. Don't judge yourself by the falls; judge yourself by the desire to get up again. Perseverance proves a person's character, not his failures.

Does he get back into the game of life? Does he give up when he stumbles? These are the questions leaders ask. What is his reaction to the blow? Can he take the abuse of the world? Is he really tough enough in head and tender enough in heart to do the job? These questions can only be answered by you.

No one can hold a first-class person down. (And no one can hold a second-class person up if he wants to be a first-class failure!)

The big question is not how many times you have been knocked down, but how many times you have gotten up. I'm convinced it's the people who get up again and again who finally end up at the top.

Get up! Failure has taught you its lesson. Now make it give you its riches. It's smart to start—again!

START TO BECOME

You will become what you must become. And whatever must be, will be by the natural laws of God. When there is a seed of life, evidence or the fruit of life will come. All sound ideas find their way to the top eventually.

What is alive, must grow. There is no way for you to be hindered permanently if what you are and what you do is sound. You will do what you must do.

As the waters flow toward the oceans, overcoming all obstacles and hindrances, so must the prayer of hope flow toward the fulfillment of things hoped for.

Delays do not kill hope; defeat will not capture it.

Despite all its woes, hope knows it cannot fail permanently. All failure is just another lesson learned by the growing person.

Hope can wait. Faith knows that what must be, will be.

Bid farewell to your ghosts and monsters. They cannot touch you or harm you. God is still at work in you. "I am sure that God who began the good work within you will keep right on helping you grow in his grace until his task within you is finally finished" (Philippians 1:6).

E L E V E N
The Tenderhearted and Tough-Minded

In this world if you can't handle turndowns when you expect things to turn up, you're out! Tough people are not crushed by the sting of sorrows. They stand up because they stand out. They refuse to crumble under the abuse of the world, but they aren't insensitive either. Let's learn from this chapter how to be both.

TOUGH BUT TENDER

You'll need to be tender **and** tough as you work toward reaching your highest potential in life.

The tender understand; the tough undertake.

The tender start; the tough keep going.

The tender find the need; the tough meet the need.

The tender dream the dream; the tough fulfill the dream.

The tender seek; the tough find.

The tender show the way; the tough lead the way.

Both qualities are needed in the person who expects to develop his fullest usefulness for God and this world.

Knowing when to be tender and when to be tough is the difference between winning and losing. Sometimes you must be tender to a person with whom, at a later time, you must be tough.

The tough-minded need tender hearts, but the tenderhearted must build tough minds. It takes a tough mind not to get hurt when sticks and stones start to fly. The tough-minded person has learned life is not a picnic. He doesn't let the people around him decide his attitude; he sets his own temperature.

Knowing who to be tender toward takes as much wisdom as knowing to whom to be tough. Jesus knew the difference. He knew when to be tough, when to be tender, and when to adjust the relationship. Studying this facet of his life will enlighten you a great deal!

The tough can say no. They understand the language of withholding themselves, protecting their time, guarding their inner person when the demanding winds start to blow. Jesus said, "Be as wary as serpents" (Matthew 10:16). He also said, "[Be] harmless as doves" (Matthew 10:16). Do you know the difference?

He also told his disciples to "Salute no man by the way" (Luke 10:4, KJV) when on an errand. There are times when we can't afford to see what every person we meet wants. An individual may want too much of you, when he really needs what can be found only in God. Point him to the Lord. You must know when to talk and when not to talk.

Be tender; be tough. Understanding the difference could make the difference in your failure or success.

DON'T BE AFRAID OF THEM

You need to know when and how to stand up for your rights. This principle is rarely taught in Sunday school. You have been taught all your life to give up, give in, turn the other cheek. All of this is good, but you also need to know when not to turn the other cheek.

If you give in too many times to the bullying of others, or yield to their insistent claims on your time and effort, you will lose your self-respect. You cannot respect yourself if you are the underdog on everybody's leash. The Bible promises you will be "the head and not the tail" (Deuteronomy 28:13). Coming in last when you could have come in first is no credit to God or you. There is no virtue in being on the losing team if you could have been on the winning team. There **is** virtue in being a good loser. But remember—if you could have been a good winner and weren't, you lost twice. This is failure.

There will be times when you must say no to your opposition. If you are going somewhere or doing something worthwhile, you **will** have opposition. But you do not have to be overcome by the opposition. Don't be pushed beyond the line of self-respect. Learn to stand up to the bullying. You might be surprised how the bully will bend if you say no to him and mean it.

Knowing when to stand up for your rights is part

of being able to find your way through life satisfactorily.

BOOST THE EGO

While my son and I were walking across the golf course one bright, spring day, he said meditatively, "You know, Dad, every leader needs an ego boost now and then. But where can he find it? He is always boosting his followers, but no one seems interested in boosting the ego of the leader."

I contemplated that statement the rest of the game as we swung our golf clubs on that beautiful, fresh day. I had never thought about the leader, the top person, needing an ego boost. I had felt the need but had not identified it. I thought being the head of a department, a home, or an organization should give enough satisfaction for anyone's ego. But my son pointed out that many highly successful men have become bitter, hard, and unruly because they lacked the encouragement that maintains self-respect and self-confidence.

The ego needs rewards. As you're developing your potential, there will be times when no one will be there to boost you or congratulate you on your achievements. The leader is expected to lead and boost all of the rest. The satisfaction he gets is seeing followers become winners. The person at the top often has no place to turn for encouragement or enlightenment. He usually is there because he encouraged himself and had the ability to light his own candle. David "encouraged himself in the Lord his God" (1 Samuel 30:6, KJV). Self-encouragement keeps you going in the face of adverse winds. If the leader lacks self-approval or self-encouragement, he will soon be at the back of the line.

Learn how to keep your ego in good repair. An unbalanced ego will unbalance your objectives and goals as well. All of life will go out of focus if you do not hang on to a healthy self-respect.

THE GOOD OF SORROW

You will meet some sorrow, heartache, and loss as you walk the road of life, But sorrow is not all bad. Pain can produce humility. It sometimes softens your approach to life.

Sorrow focuses your eyes more sharply on your goals. It brings you back to your true self. It teaches you to comfort others as others have comforted you (see 2 Corinthians 1:4).

Sorrow drains off the slush. It keeps you serious about life and its purpose.

The greatest lesson you can learn from sorrow is to be thankful for it. The Bible commands us, "No matter what happens, always be thankful" (1 Thessalonians 5:18). A giant step toward being the "unlimited you" will come about as you thank God for the sorrow. The healing of wounds is found in the medication of praise.

As you praise God for loss, disappointment, and sorrow, it seems to heal and blossom into something new. You can rise above a situation only by praise.

Once sorrow has done its work, its pain will move out of your life. It will melt away, thus making room for more growth.

You will always have sorrow, but learning to

109

handle it by praise turns it to good in your life. You may never understand the reason for sorrow, but praise will remove its remorse.

You have God's presence, his promises, and the prayers of God's people around the world working for you. Sorrow can light up your life or turn it off. The choice is yours.

LITTLE PEOPLE NEED BIG THINGS

Little people need big things to prove they are somebody.

Little people need the approval and acceptance of the "in-group" to feel they are worthwhile.

The weaker the ego, the greater the compliment must be. The weak self-image seeks center stage in others' spotlights. It is afraid to put on its own show or produce its own play.

The weak need the strong to lead, guide, and provide for them. The weak will sacrifice their persons, their hopes, and their dreams if the strong will only give them a place in the sun.

The weak have forgotten that a place in the sun is not a gift—it is earned by effort. They are hoping to fall in line with the parade and be in the band even though they cannot play the music, enjoy the tune, or keep in step. They hide in the crowd and so cover up the fears and insecurities that plague them.

The weak flee when someone speaks against them; they cannot stand criticism. Their world falls apart at the frown of a friend.

They live like a baby in a crib, crying for comfort; but when the cold hand of opposition or resistance touches them, they turn into a tormented child. The only safe place is under the covers. They would rather spend their entire lives undercover, approved and protected, than grow up and climb out of the crib.

These are the people you must deal with as you seek to reach your best potential.

MISPLACED BECAUSE YOU'RE MISUNDERSTOOD

No person ever feels he is fully understood or loved as he longs to be. You will often feel the need to be cared for and approved. A smile from a stranger, a little favor from a passerby, brings joy to your heart because you feel another's support.

Whoever understands you has unlimited value to you. When you are undergirded emotionally, mentally, or spiritually by someone else, that person becomes indispensable to you.

You will never be alone if you seek to understand others. Take the time to listen, feel, and lift up a neighbor. The world will beat a path to your door if you do. The businesses, homes, and churches that are flourishing most are the places where people feel understood and loved.

Do unto others what you want from others. Everybody is important, and the greatest need in the hearts of people is that someone might understand and accept them as they seek to develop their unlimited selves.

The person who is not loved or understood chooses one of three paths: (1) He becomes hard, (2) he becomes indifferent, or (3) he quits. There is no sadder individual than the one who is misunderstood and who then becomes a misfit in the world of events.

You may never feel you are fully understood or loved as you wish to be. (In reality only Christ can meet this need.) But the pains, the frustrations, and the battles of your life could knock you down unless you are building inner resources to withstand the attack.

Don't turn back when the going gets rough—turn on! "If God be for you, everybody else might as well be," said an intelligent little boy.

HAVE YOU BEEN MISREAD?

You will be misunderstood many times as your unlimited potential unfolds. You will be misread. The signals you give off will be "out-of-phase." Rejection by others will become evident many times.

Being misunderstood can be part of maturing. Each time you grow and change, you will be misunderstood and misread by old associates. They know you as you **were.** They often don't want to know you as you **are becoming. Becoming** separates.

But such separation is only for a season. At times it will seem that all have abandoned you. These will be dark moments in your life, and you will face the temptation to give up and give in just to gain acceptance. But, misunderstood or not, you must continue on your path of truth, honesty, and the fulfillment of your dreams.

Jesus was misread by his family, friends, and the age in which he lived. Whenever you reach beyond the ordinary, you **will** be misread. But if your goals are good, workable, and useful to the world, people will reach for you eventually.

First comes rejection, then reception.

It is between the two that most people give up. The ability to go from **rejection** to **reception** makes the difference in what you achieve. Once you understand the motivation that can come from misunderstanding, you will move toward your potential. Use misunderstanding to motivate you to a stronger purpose in your walk with God.

TWELVE
Need Is Supply Knocking

Big needs are big supplies wanting to enter your life. You only experience the supplies you require if you make room for them by recognizing needs. The pantry is full, but you must use the key of giving to unlock the door.

THE KEY TO THE SUPPLY ROOM

Wherever there is a need, it calls to the supply. Thirst calls for water; hunger calls for food; sickness calls for healing.

Your objective is to find a method through which supply can come. The fish are in the sea. The question is, how do you get them into your boat? Jesus found some fishermen with empty nets. As far as these men were concerned, the sea was empty as well. After Jesus used their boat, he said, "Now go out where it is deeper and let down your nets and you will catch a lot of fish" (Luke 5:4). They had given; now he would give.

Here is the key that unlocks the door of need. The disciples gave Christ their empty boat, and now he gave them a full boat. Giving is the secret.

Need is waiting for supply, and supply will respond to the act of giving. But supply will give to you only if you have given to another's need.

What can you give? Let the size of your need determine the size of your giving, for this will determine the size of the supply.

Let giving become a way of life, and you will receive more than you need.

GIVE WHAT YOU NEED

The door to abundant receiving is found in generous giving. Learning to give at all times is the secret of receiving at all times. Never look to anyone to give to you; see who you can help.

This is God's formula for supply and for happiness. It cannot be denied, delayed, or defeated.

Whatever you need, give some of it away. At first this will seem senseless. But keep at it, with only the thought of giving. The receiving will come. It may come from hidden sources, but it will come, as surely as day follows night.

Give to those whom you don't like. Give with no strings attached. Giving for Christ's sake will produce the gain you need.

Need is a seed, and your potential is locked up in your need. Give as Christ gave, and you'll soon have more than you need. Giving multiplies what you already have.

GIVING IS RECEIVING

Paul and Nancy Olson, a beautiful young couple with a sweet little girl, have a growing construction company. One Saturday night the Lord spoke to Nancy and said, "I want you to give the church $1,000 tomorrow."

She told me, "I nearly fainted." The winter had been long, and the money had been short.

She said, "Lord, I will give the money if Pastor asks the people for $1,000." She felt safe with that type of covenant because I had not mentioned money in such a way for a long time. My associates had taken the responsibility of asking for the finances and raising the money.

But that beautiful Sunday morning as I stood to preach, I related to the people that we had a need for blacktopping. I needed twenty people who would give $1,000 each. Nancy nearly fainted again. I had requested exactly what she had promised to give the Lord!

The Olsons wrote the check and gave it to the Lord.

About three weeks had gone by when Nancy came to me, thrilled and excited, and said, "You remember when we gave that $1,000? Well, this week we received an unexpected check for $5,000."

I wept, she wept, and we both rejoiced!

When you give, Christ always does more than you ask or even think. Christ did **five** times more for Paul and Nancy that day.

EXPECTATIONS BUILD EXPERIENCES

You must expect an increase if you are to see a return on your giving. As you work with God and his laws, anticipate results. Many people pray but don't expect. Some give but don't really believe there will be results from their giving.

It is not wrong to expect a return on your efforts of faith. "Give generously, for your gifts will return to you later" (Ecclesiastes 11:1).

Let expectancy be a conscious thing in you. Watch for the returns. Say to yourself, "I expect answers to prayer. I expect good to come to me."

Affirm these expectations daily. What you expect is vital, because in most cases you get what you expect—good or bad.

All things you expect come from God—if you expect the best. Friends come from God. Love comes from God. Faith comes from God.

And you can expect the best if you are giving the best.

Always expect the Lord to be good to you. Your expectations govern your world, and your foremost goal should be to daily build the power of expectation.

Expect and you will experience.

EVERYONE NEEDS APPROVAL

Everyone needs approval, but needing too much approval can be crippling. Needing too much of it is a sign of weak self-esteem. When you have developed high self-esteem, others' approval will be less important to you.

A low self-image creates voracious needs for acceptance and approval. Athletes fail, politicians quit, and families fall apart because they have an abnormal need to be appreciated. Limit the number of

117

people in your life from whom you desire approval. Paul said he was approved of the Lord, and that this was even greater than being approved by his brethren. God said about Jesus, "This is my beloved Son, and I am wonderfully pleased with him" (Matthew 3:17).

You are accepted in the Beloved (Ephesians 1:6). Who else's acceptance do you really need?

When there is too much dependence on parents or peers for approval, there is a tendency to compromise your ambitions. Once you learn to be satisfied with what you are doing, who you are, and how you treat other people, the approval of others will seem less necessary to you. Trying to find too many people to be happy with you will keep you unhappy. Don't depend on others to make you happy. Find happiness within, where Christ lives.

Don't depend on others to motivate you to success. That, too, must come from within you. No one will prepare your speeches or pray your prayers. If you are to be effective, you will need to express what you think clearly and who you are confidently. Any other image will be marked "Reject." Don't develop a large appetite for approval. You just might starve to death emotionally.

And finally, if you have a need for approval, give it.

BIG NEEDS DEMAND RISK

There will never be a time when you will not have a need.

Every human being is in need from birth to death. He needs love, food, understanding, money, and a thousand more things.

118

This generation has needs, the last generation had needs, and the coming generation will have needs. And God is never finished supplying the needs in every generation for every person who trusts him.

A widow mentioned in the Bible had a big need. She had only enough food for one day for herself and her son; then they would face death. The prophet Elijah had needs too. He had to find food or he too would die.

Each of them had something to give. If she would give food, Elijah would give faith. She was asked to give what little she had. To make matters worse, she was to give it to Elijah, who had no way of returning it. And she was to give the food to him first!

Insanity? Maybe. But she obeyed.

First, she gave what she had. This was not a loss, for at the point of giving, a miracle took place. Where there had been none, there was now more than enough. This miracle fed the family and the prophet for over a year (see 1 Kings 17:10-16).

Nothing is ever lost by giving. She risked what she had, Elijah risked what he had, and both of them received more of what they gave. Faith and food became evident in that house. The spiritual responded to the material when the two were joined by faith.

HOARDING LEADS TO POVERTY

The way to riches is reached through the gate of giving. You can only get a return on what you give. Hoarding money will lead to poverty of spirit, friendship, soul, and perhaps of money itself.

According to the Bible, withholding money that belongs to God will leave holes in your pocket (see Haggai 1:6). You will lose your money, hardly knowing where it went, if you withhold it when it should be shared.

Would you like to have plenty of money? Then give. There are multitudes of books on how to get rich. Most of them tell you how to get; the Bible tells you how to give. It says you gain wealth by giving.

Luke 6:38 tells us, "If you give, you will get." If you have a need, plant a seed. Plant the very thing you need. And don't look for the harvest, but release even the anticipated return.

When you sow a thing, let it go. There is no controlling the seed once it is planted. You must not seek to control your money once you give it. Plant it out of your reach.

Let giving become a way of life. Give to all. Be as free as God is in his giving. Have you ever noticed how freely he gives to all? He even gives to people you don't like.

Riches come to the abundant giver. What a harvest you will reap as you freely give everything you own.

T H I R T E E N
Who's Who in the World of What's What

Knowing who's who in the world of what's what will take some undertaking and understanding. Understanding your own world helps in understanding the whole world in general, for you are a little part of the big whole. Your self-image may be disfigured by the complexities of life in this century, but it can be reconstructed by self-denial, keeping a free spirit, and never living to prove a point. Live to prove a life! Let's see how these concepts unfold.

WHO ARE YOU?

What you accomplish in life is determined by **who** you are. It is never determined by **what** you are. When you know who you are, you will know what to do in life and how to do it.

Knowing yourself helps you to understand yourself. The confused person is crippled in mind, imagination, and initiative. Knowing who you are untangles such confusion.

Whatever God has started in you, he will carry to completion. He may allow you to pass through many trials and testings, but there will be a victor's trophy in this world and in the world to come.

Pressures teach you who you are. Are you listening?

Pressures also push you to find the unlimited. You will never know how much you can do or become until pressures press you into action. In your doing, you grow into your being.

Most of your growth is a result of your groans. So the pain of growing is rewarding, if you will endure it.

Look behind your problems to divine providence, and you will have it made. Don't stare into evil; stare through it to God.

The "unlimited you" is always developing. Use your experiences to build an example of life with unlimited possibilities.

The problems will be real. The limiting situations will be difficult. But remember: the unlimited life is developing in you. The pressures and limitations you face are moving your life toward growth and expansion.

Your problems can bring progress!

JESUS DIDN'T COME TO PROVE A POINT

Asking, "What would Jesus do?" is not as childlike as you may think. The only perfect man, the only person who had it all together, was Jesus. He is a worthy example for you to follow.

Learn how Jesus worked and prayed (and how

he died) and you will have the hidden secret of all true success.

He conquered on natural and spiritual planes, and left the same ability with you in the power of his Holy Spirit. He transferred his power to you by his Spirit.

Study the life of Jesus. But don't study him to prove a point. Study him to live a life. The greatest proof that you are right in what you believe is what you are becoming.

Jesus never came to prove a point. He came to give life—abundant life. The next time you are pressed by twentieth-century problems, take a long look at the timeless figure of Jesus; then imitate him.

You will never be the perfect Christ, but you can have the perfect Christ working fully in you. The more freedom you allow him in your life, the closer you will come to your unlimited potential.

Make room for Jesus. Don't substitute anything for him. He's the key to the whole point of life.

WATCH OUT FOR SELF-REJECTION

One of the biggest hurdles you need to overcome while developing an unlimited personality is self-rejection. I believe a lack of self-acceptance is the cruelest of all taskmasters. This attitude may take on the form of guilt, condemnation, or self-hate.

Self-rejection wounds the spirit and causes the soul to bleed. The mind cannot function as intended when the spirit is wounded.

The Bible says, "When courage dies, what hope

123

is left?" (Proverbs 18:14). You must seek to build faith in what you are doing and where you are going. The basis for all successful achievement is self-improvement in what you are and what you're accomplishing.

Don't worry about living **on** much; only be concerned about living **for** much. You have much to live for.

Self-rejection or low self-esteem will destroy your progress and your personal relationships with others. Influencing others comes from the power of self-acceptance. When you really like yourself, it will be easy to like others.

People who are hateful are full of self-hate, though it is often hidden by an overbearing manner, snobbery, or complete withdrawal.

The road to success becomes easier when you truly accept yourself. This frees you from seeking to conform in order to gain acceptance. Conforming becomes not a matter of acceptance, but of convenience. If it's better for the team, then conform. But if the conformation is self-destructive, refuse it.

You're always more important for what you **are** than for what you do.

HOW JEALOUSY FOUND REALITY

We did not see Maxine and her husband in the restaurant, but they saw us. The restaurant was filled with people eating breakfast. People were coming and going as my wife and I sat conversing and eating a delightful breakfast.

This couple watched us all through the meal. The joy of Christ caught their attention, and they wanted what they saw in us. Less than a month later they found the secret to this full life in Jesus. What they longed for, they now possess.

What do you have that's real? Has anybody envied your relationship to God and your ability to handle life? Who's looking at you today with a desire to have what you have?

All true virtue is unknown to the possessor. This is what makes it work. The sun is not conscious of itself, nor are the stars. They just shine. When you are aware of a virtue, it ceases to exist. If you are humble, you will be the last one to recognize it. The only thing you need to know is that you are alive in Christ.

Reality is found in Jesus Christ. Go to the Source, and you will have all.

THE DISFIGURED IMAGE

When were you happiest?

At what point on life's road were you really in control?

Examine your history. Locate the chapter and page where you shone in all your self-respect. Find out if your roots lead back to righteousness and goodness. Remember the days or years when you felt able to succeed. Go back to that point; relive it in your mind.

Like the clear-cut outline of granite, your image can become disfigured because of years of battling the elements. Reconstruct the true you.

The storms, temptations, rejections, and general abuse of the world can disfigure your original image. Occasionally sit down and recount the bright spots.

Pull down from the attic of your mind the old, dusty "self album" and get out the pictures of you when you were at your best. Don't let these hopes or solid images fade. You may need to adjust some of these hopes and dreams because of the turn of events. But keep the glow of the real you in view.

As he walked for forty years through the wilderness with an unruly bunch of slaves, Moses was instructed, "Build your life in the valley according to what you saw on the mountain." The valleys can easily make you forget the mountaintops.

Keep your blueprint by your side when you're building in the mud. The mud pile could become the place where you blossom like a rose.

Go back. Then go on!

DENY YOURSELF

Self-denial is difficult, but to never deny yourself is to never discover yourself. Having all you want when you want it may look exciting, but it will mar your true person.

One of the doors to unlimited supply is the door of self-denial. Deny yourself the freedom to live as you like or as you please. You can do a lot of things which are not sinful, but which lock the doors to the unlimited because they spring from pleasing only yourself.

There is much talk about loving yourself. But Jesus also spoke about denying yourself, taking up your cross, and following him. Self-denial is a must. If you truly want to find your true person, lose yourself in a cause bigger than yourself. If you lose your life, you will find it (see Matthew 10:39).

It's hard to deny yourself. And as you practice self-denial, you will be looked upon and pitied by many. But do it anyway.

Deny yourself so God's best plans for you can take place in your life. Self-denial keeps the channels open for a stream of good things.

Denial in itself brings no power. It is directed denial, self-denial with a purpose, that brings power.

Take the cross, though many will not. The cross will lead you to a crown of life's joys.

You will understand who's who in a world of what's what as you seek to sort out the good from the best, the urgent from the important. Self-denial is like putting savings in the bank. It draws interest. There are some things better left undone now, so you won't have to undo them in the future.

FREE SPIRIT

Let the world take your silver and gold, but don't let it touch your spirit, for here all your abilities lie. A godly spirit sustains you in the situation of sorrow. If your spirit is crushed or captured, your hopes and abilities will die. If your spirit is held in bondage through threats of isolation or destruction of its free-flowing ideas and big dreams, the production of new worlds will cease.

Freedom is necessary for dreamers, poets, and prophets to express what they see or perceive; otherwise progress will come to a standstill.

This is why Russia puts restrictions on its dreamers. All rigid systems must crush the creator, or there might be a revelation which would liberate the minds of others.

We salute the people of yesterday who brought our breakthroughs. But sadly we also execute or at least hinder those who are seeking to bring a breakthrough today. Yesterday's thinkers are respected, and it is dangerous to reject today's seekers.

Seek freedom of the spirit. The spirit of the believer **will** triumph. It cannot be destroyed or defeated.

No one can capture or imprison your spirit. The spirit knows, the spirit grows, the spirit flows. With God's help, the spirit of a man unlocks the secrets of the universe.

When you are free in spirit, all other freedoms will follow in time.

HOW DO YOU SEE YOURSELF?

How you see yourself is more important than how others see you. You will achieve your dreams if you believe you can. Many people will limit you, but you will know when you feel the potential of an unlimited you developing.

People limit you because of the image they saw of you in the past. Your changing or growing is a challenge to them. Then too, the image which they hold of you may come from their own low self-esteem; they may be venting their feelings in your direction.

I had a neighbor who was very angry at the church. Nothing pleased him. When he later got a divorce, I understood why he took revenge on the church. If I had believed his image of us as a church, I would have soon been trapped. Time proved which of us had the wrong image.

Your self-image is vital to you. A good image can accept failure or success without affecting the true person. You will learn both to be content with much or little, like the Apostle Paul, without going to pieces (Philippians 4).

Your self-image is not based primarily on accomplishments, but on attitude. Debbie Boone said after selling four and a half million records, "I don't need success to make me happy." She had a sound self-image long before she hit the big time. Perhaps this very picture of herself caused the big time to happen.

What we are, we attract—if we can handle the attraction.

Start today to thank God for you. Try it. Don't wish you didn't exist.

Be willing to grow with yourself. Be thankful you are you. This is the starting place to becoming the person you want to be.

Understanding and accepting yourself is the first step toward the unlimited you. It's vital that you see yourself in the true light. That's far more important than how anyone else sees you.

FOURTEEN
Hangovers Come from Hang-Ups

It seems the easiest thing in the world is to get hang-ups, which usually come from bang-ups. Somewhere you have had a blow from an enemy or even a friend. Somebody has cut you to the core. Maybe you have been misunderstood or misrepresented. This caused you to start ducking your head when you were around other people. You felt you were a marked bird. You thought everyone was taking a potshot at you. A hang-up like this is the start of an attitude of failure. It will bring more misery into your life than you can handle. In time you'll probably determine your only escape is to run away.

Most hang-ups start from some apparently uncontrollable attitude. But in reality the devil or people can do no more with you than you allow them to do in your mind. If the mind is crippled by false illusions, fearful speculations, and lack of creative imagination, you will get a real hang-up. And a hang-up can soon become a hangover.

Hangovers come out of the past. Attitudes, resentments, and disappointments that have never been touched by the healing love of Jesus Christ become hangovers. Unresolved hang-ups soon become hangovers.

Is it possible to live without hang-ups? I believe Jesus wants you free from these hurtful reactions. His people should be whole people, though at times it seems like the religious have more hang-ups than the nonreligious.

I think most of us take on more restrictions than necessary and open ourselves to unnecessary rebuffs. Self-imposed restrictions usually cause us to have hang-ups. When we don't chase hangovers away, they become hang-ups, and then we are in danger of losing our liberty, joy, and self-acceptance.

Live with Christ, taking full advantage of his freedom. Give up the hangovers and the hang-ups produced by the bang-ups of life. You might be surprised just how quickly you will grow when the hang-ups have been given over to Christ, though there will still be times when life seems unfair.

IT ALL SEEMS SO UNFAIR

Life **is** often unfair! Life is not guaranteed to be a rose garden. Life must be lived.

You will think life is unfair a million times before you die:

1. You were born at the wrong time in history.
2. Your parents were poor or divorced.
3. Your family was not close.
4. The other kids at school got all the breaks.

131

5. Your teeth were crooked.
6. Your best girlfriend married your best boyfriend.
7. The car you drive always develops a rattle or a knock.
8. A low-income neighborhood develops around the house you live in and lowers the value of your property.
9. Your husband is never at home when you need him.
10. Your wife does not understand your sexual needs.
11. The boss at the office shows favoritism.
12. God seems to favor others and ignore your needs.

It all seems so unfair—and it is.

You will think something must have gone wrong in your heritage or your genes. But the situation might be the unwelcome will of God, forcing you to live this way and teaching you humility.

Jacob cried out in his blinded grief, "Everything has been against me" (Genesis 42:36). All he could see were the things that were against him. The story could have ended here, but God graciously turned the page and opened a new chapter.

In the new chapter Joseph, the son Jacob favored, the son he thought had been destroyed by a wild animal, was now the prime minister of the greatest country in the world. All was **for** Jacob, but he thought all was **against** him.

Jacob didn't see or understand how the "bad" things in his life were good things in disguise. Jacob reasoned, "All is against me," but God had not abandoned his servant.

How is your eyesight?

ARE YOU UP AGAINST IT?

Have you ever felt like Jacob? Nothing is going your way. Every way you turn, you are threatened by foes who hinder you and friends who pity you. You conclude, as Jacob did, "Everything has been against me."

Jacob felt the same way when he faced the loss of Joseph, his favorite son. There was a famine in the Promised Land, and loneliness hit him at old age. There was not a trace of encouragement anywhere to be found in the life of Jacob. The past hope of the Promised Land was overgrown with weeds. He found no path to peace or prosperity. It seemed life would end on a sour note for Jacob. The sun would set on the tired, beaten, and hurting heart of the old man.

Meeting God at Peniel (where he had seen the angels and where God had changed his name to Israel) didn't seem to turn out as he had planned. Either his prayers were misdirected or he had misread the message. Something wasn't working at this time in Jacob's life. The only conclusion he could muster was, "All these things are against me. I must have made a mistake."

He is not alone in that hasty conclusion. You have felt it a thousand times yourself:

1. Prayer seems prevented.
2. Hope seems hindered.
3. Your friends flee.
4. The foes stay.

What's the use?

But within the troubles of Jacob a divine hand was still at work.

The hurt God allowed compelled Jacob to find a bigger life. Joseph had to be hated in order to find a greater people. Delays were God's appointed ways of bringing a much greater deliverance.

Jacob finally saw it. His son was loved and lord over all of Egypt. There was no more shortage, no more sorrows for Jacob. The things against him were, in reality, **for** him.

Jacob waited long enough to prove that circumstances lie. There was a Providence bigger than his problem. From that point on Jacob was never up against it again. He closed his life in the sunset of his brightest dreams.

His hangovers were finally hung up like an old sword that had won the victory against all that came against him. But remember, it was his problem which led later to the security of God's people.

NO PROBLEMS, NO PROGRESS

Your problems will push you into action if you let them. All problems solved mean all progress has ceased, and you have settled for second-best.

God started with chaos, then created the cosmos. You, too, often start with chaos. Beginning is usually hard. The positive side does not lead to the negative; the negative brings out the positive. A dark background emphasizes a light foreground. Contrast in colors makes for a brighter picture.

Problems are producers. No problems, no

prayers. No problems, no creativity. My best prayers and most helpful books came in times of the deepest troubles.

When you have to struggle to survive, you will survive, while the comfortable and frozen are soon in the company of the dead. Lukewarmness makes God sick to his stomach (see Revelation 3:16).

The meaning of joy cannot be found in joy, but in sorrow. Each time you face a meaningless situation, you are on the edge of a fresh discovery. The **whys** of life lead to the **ways** and **hows** of life.

When you feel all is in control, you are about to lose the sharp edge. Dullness settles in when a knife has no resistance to sharpen its blade.

Paul cried out, "I am glad to boast about how weak I am; I am glad to be a living demonstration of Christ's power . . ." (2 Corinthians 12:9). Paul turned his infirmities into opportunities for grace and glory to shine through. Paul's hang-ups were teaching him to turn his troubles to trophies.

HOW TO TRANSFORM YOUR TROUBLES

Learn to rejoice in your troubles. Paul welcomed his infirmities. The power to transcend your troubles is the power of praise. The more you thank God for trials, the more he delivers you from them.

The world is no easy place in which to live. All kinds of trouble, problems, and temptations confront you everyday. You will have your share of difficulties as you unfold the plans of your dreams.

Everyone has problems. The secret is to thank God for them if you expect to live above them. They will gall you and make you bitter and resentful if you don't praise him for them.

The first step in transforming your troubles is to see them as useful. Their usefulness may not be clear to your mind at the present. You may not understand the trouble or see how it is working for you at the moment.

But faith in the goodness of God does not require you to understand. Praise him for the things you don't understand. Let the Great Designer decide the outcome of your life's situations.

All leaders face mountains of troubles. One reason you love to read the Bible is because you find people like yourself who triumphed over their problems. The Bible is a recipe book full of people's experiences. Follow their example, and you will discover their victory.

Give praise for your troubles and they will, in time, come back to you as trophies. While the unlimited is developing, you will find that all your disadvantages were useful to you.

DISADVANTAGES ARE USEFUL

There was a man in the Bible who had a withered hand. It was useless. Perhaps the disability came about through a birth defect, some accident, or a disease. Whatever, the hand was withered.

While you are growing into your potential, there will be many times when you will discover that your "hand" is withered or crushed. You may be crippled by a slight remark, a word of criticism, a deed which someone has done against you and your good intentions. An accident of life could land you in a physical or spiritual wheelchair. Your hopes could be shriveled or in shambles. The fruit on your vine could wither.

You will be faced with withered circumstances and situations many times.

1. The hand of faith will shrivel.
2. The hand of success will dry up.
3. The dreams you put so much stock in will explode in your face.

Only the strong go on in times like those.

You must take hold of your disadvantages and use them. The thing which is causing you the most discomfort today, the greatest heartache, tears, and agony, could very well be the hidden key that could unlock your greatest tomorrows. Today's withering could be the beginning of bringing your paralyzed condition into full blooms of new life and growth.

Trouble works two ways: it can send you under or over. Your interpretation of it and reaction to it make all the difference.

Jesus healed that man's withered hand. What the man did with it after it was healed, we are not told. I hope when you find the solution to your problems, you will let the world know what you did with your withered hand made whole by Christ.

Your hangovers and hang-ups can be cleared up by the touch of Christ. But don't let it stop there. Take the message of your healing to others who are hurting and are looking for a way through this withered world!

Other Living Books Bestsellers

THE BEST CHRISTMAS PAGEANT EVER by Barbara Robinson. A delightfully wild and funny story about what can happen to a Christmas program when the "horrible Herdman" family of brothers and sisters are miscast in the roles of the Christmas story characters from the Bible. 07–0137 $2.50.

ELIJAH by William H. Stephens. He was a rough-hewn farmer who strolled onto the stage of history to deliver warnings to Ahab the king and to defy Jezebel the queen. A powerful biblical novel you will never forget. 07–4023 $3.95.

THE TOTAL MAN by Dan Benson. A practical guide on how to gain confidence and fulfillment. Covering areas such as budgeting of time, money matters, and marital relationships. 07–7289 $3.50.

HOW TO HAVE ALL THE TIME YOU NEED EVERY DAY by Pat King. Drawing from her own and other women's experiences as well as from the Bible and the research of time experts, Pat has written a warm and personal book for every Christian woman. 07–1529 $3.50.

IT'S INCREDIBLE by Ann Kiemel. "It's incredible" is what some people say when a slim young woman says, "Hi, I'm Ann," and starts talking about love and good and beauty. As Ann tells about a Jesus who can make all the difference in their lives, some call that incredible, and turn away. Others become miracles themselves, agreeing with Ann that it's incredible. 07–1818 $2.50.

THE PEPPERMINT GANG AND THE EVERGEEN CASTLE by Laurie Clifford. A heartwarming story about the growing pains of five children whose hilarious adventures teach them unforgettable lessons about love and forgiveness, life and death. Delightful reading for all ages. 07–0779 $3.50.

JOHN, SON OF THUNDER by Ellen Gunderson Traylor. Travel with John down the desert paths, through the courts of the Holy City, and to the foot of the cross. Journey with him from his luxury as a privileged son of Israel to the bitter hardship of his exile on Patmos. This is a saga of adventure, romance, and discovery—of a man bigger than life—the disciple "whom Jesus loved." 07–1903 $3.95.

WHAT'S IN A NAME? compiled by Linda Francis, John Hartzel, and Al Palmquist. A fascinating name dictionary that features the literal meaning of people's first names, the character quality implied by the name, and an applicable Scripture verse for each name listed. Ideal for expectant parents! 07–7935 $2.95.

Other Living Books Bestsellers

THE MAN WHO COULD DO NO WRONG by Charles E. Blair with John and Elizabeth Sherrill. He built one of the largest churches in America . . . then he made a mistake. This is the incredible story of Pastor Charles E. Blair, accused of massive fraud. A book "for error-prone people in search of the Christian's secret for handling mistakes." 07–4002 $3.50.

GIVERS, TAKERS AND OTHER KINDS OF LOVERS by Josh McDowell. This book bypasses vague generalities about love and sex and gets right down to basic questions: Whatever happened to sexual freedom? What's true love like? What is your most important sex organ? Do men respond differently than women? If you're looking for straight answers about God's plan for love and sexuality then this book was written for you. 07–1031 $2.50.

MORE THAN A CARPENTER by Josh McDowell. This best selling author thought Christians must be "out of their minds." He put them down. He argued against their faith. But eventually he saw that his arguments wouldn't stand up. In this book, Josh focuses upon the person who changed his life—Jesus Christ. 07–4552 $2.50.

HIND'S FEET ON HIGH PLACES by Hannah Hurnard. A classic allegory which has sold more than a million copies! 07–1429 $3.50.

THE CATCH ME KILLER by Bob Erler with John Souter. Golden gloves, black bell, green beret, silver badge. Supercop Bob Erler had earned the colors of manhood. Now can he survive prison life? An incredible true story of forgiveness and hope. 07–0214 $3.50.

WHAT WIVES WISH THEIR HUSBANDS KNEW ABOUT WOMEN by Dr. James Dobson. By the best selling author of *DARE TO DISCIPLINE* and *THE STRONG-WILLED CHILD,* here's a vital book that speaks to the unique emotional needs and aspirations of today's woman. An immensely practical, interesting guide. 07–7896 $2.95.

PONTIUS PILATE by Dr. Paul Maier. This fascinating novel is about one of the most famous Romans in history—the man who declared Jesus innocent but who nevertheless sent him to the cross. This powerful biblical novel gives you a unique insight into the life and death of Jesus. 07–4852 $3.95.

LIFE IS TREMENDOUS by Charlie Jones. Believing that enthusiasm makes the difference, Jones shows how anyone can be happy, involved, relevant, productive, healthy, and secure in the midst of a high-pressure, commercialized, automated society. 07–2184 $2.50.

HOW TO BE HAPPY THOUGH MARRIED by Dr. Tim LaHaye. One of America's most successful marriage counselors gives practical, proven advice for marital happiness. 07–1499 $2.95.

Other Living Books Bestsellers

DAVID AND BATHSHEBA by Roberta Kells Dorr. Was Bathsheba an innocent country girl or a scheming adulteress? What was King David really like? Solomon—the wisest man in the world—was to be king, but could he survive his brothers' intrigues? Here is an epic love story which comes radiantly alive through the art of a fine storyteller. 07–0618 $4.50.

TOO MEAN TO DIE by Nick Pirovolos with William Proctor. In this action-packed story, Nick the Greek tells how he grew from a scrappy immigrant boy to a fearless underworld criminal. Finally caught, he was imprisoned. But something remarkable happened and he was set free—truly set free! 07–7283 $3.95.

FOR WOMEN ONLY. This bestseller gives a balanced, entertaining, diversified treatment of all aspects of womanhood. Edited by Evelyn and J. Allan Petersen, founder of Family Concern. 07–0897 $3.95.

FOR MEN ONLY. Edited by J. Allan Petersen, this book gives solid advice on how men can cope with the tremendous pressures they face every day as fathers, husbands, workers. 07–0892 $3.50.

ROCK. What is rock music really doing to you? Bob Larson presents a well-researched and penetrating look at today's rock music and rock performers. What are lyrics really saying? Who are the top performers and what are their life-styles? 07–5686 $2.95.

THE ALCOHOL TRAP by Fred Foster. A successful film executive was about to lose everything—his family's vacation home, his house in New Jersey, his reputation in the film industry, his wife. This is an emotion-packed story of hope and encouragement, offering valuable insights into the troubled world of high pressure living and alcoholism. 07–0078 $2.95.

LET ME BE A WOMAN. Best selling author Elisabeth Elliot (author of *THROUGH GATES OF SPLENDOR*) presents her profound and unique perspective on womanhood. This is a significant book on a continuing controversial subject. 07–2162 $3.50.

WE'RE IN THE ARMY NOW by Imeldia Morris Eller. Five children become their older brother's "army" as they work together to keep their family intact during a time of crisis for their mother. 07–7862 $2.95.

WILD CHILD by Mari Hanes. A heartrending story of a young boy who was abandoned and struggled alone for survival. You will be moved as you read how one woman's love tames this boy who was more animal than human. 07–8224 $2.95.

THE SURGEON'S FAMILY by David Hernandez with Carole Gift Page. This is an incredible three-generation story of a family that has faced danger and death—and has survived. Walking dead-end streets of violence and poverty, often seemingly without hope, the family of David Hernandez has struggled to find a new kind of life. 07–6684 $2.95.

The books listed are available at your bookstore. If unavailable, send check with order to cover retail price plus 10% for postage and handling to:

Tyndale House Publishers, Inc.
Box 80
Wheaton, Illinois 60189

Prices and availability subject to change without notice.
Allow 4–6 weeks for delivery.